THE THIRLWAY JOURNAL

A Record of Life in Early Victorian Ripon

Henry Steel Thirlway and his wife in old age.

THE THIRLWAY JOURNAL
A Record of Life In Early Victorian Ripon

Editor
Jean Denton

Foreword by
R. H. Thirlway

Copyright: Jean Denton
and Ripon Historical Society

ISBN No 1 872618 26 X

Published by
Ripon Historical Society
and Ripon, Harrogate and District
Family History Group

Designed and printed by
Maxiprint,
York, England

CONTENTS

List of Illustrations … … … … … … … … … … … … … …vi

Foreword by R.H.Thirlway … … … … … … … … … … …vii

Acknowledgements … … … … … … … … … … … … …viii

Introduction … … … … … … … … … … … … … … …ix

1. The Family … … … … … … … … … … … … … … …1

2. The Business … … … … … … … … … … … … … …14

3. Religion … … … … … … … … … … … … … … …23

4. Mechanics Institute … … … … … … … … … … … …29

5. Railways … … … … … … … … … … … … … … …34

6. Celebrations … … … … … … … … … … … … … …45

7. Entertainment … … … … … … … … … … … … …55

8. Weather and Social Conditions … … … … … … … …62

9. Politics and Local Administration … … … … … … …66

10. Holidays and Excursions … … … … … … … … … …73

11. People … … … … … … … … … … … … … … …91

12. Miscellaneous Events … … … … … … … … … … …97

13. Mary Jane's Diary … … … … … … … … … … … …104

Notes … … … … … … … … … … … … … … … …111

Index to People … … … … … … … … … … … … …120

Index to Places … … … … … … … … … … … … …125

LIST OF ILLUSTRATIONS

Plate — *Page*

Thirlway's Corner as reconstructed by the diarist's great-grandson from late Victorian photographs. — Front Cover

Genealogical Table showing members of the Thirlway family mentioned in the journal. — Inside Front Cover

Henry Steel Thirlway and his wife in old age. — Frontispiece

1. An account believed to be the first order of stock made by Henry Thirlway, the diarist's father, when he set up his business in Middle Street, Ripon, in 1809. — 3

2. Jepson's Hospital, the school in Water Skellgate where the diarist received his education. — 4

3. Journal open at the account of the diarist's wedding. — 10 and 11

4. Thirlway's Corner in the late Victorian period. The diarist is standing in the doorway. — 15

5. The Right Reverend Charles Thomas Longley, D.D., first Bishop of Ripon. — 24

6. Ripon Minster as shown on Thirlway notepaper mentioned in the journal. — 27

7. The Leeds and Thirsk Railway in Ripon. — 35

8. Local railways used by the diarist. — 37

9. A 20th century steam train crosses the Ure railway viaduct, the building of which is described in the journal. — 39

10. Wilfrid Festival in Kirkgate, 1844 (London Illustrated News). — 47

11. Poster calling a meeting to discuss Ripon's celebrations for Queen Victoria's Coronation. — 51

12. Tory poster printed by Henry Thirlway in 1834. — 67

13. Ripon Market Place with the Town Hall (Mrs Lawrence's Hall), 1837.

14. Temperance Society leaflet distributed in London at the time of the execution of Good, the murderer, as mentioned in the diarist's account of his visit to the capital. Leaflet fixed in the journal. — 82

15. Portrait of Mrs Lawrence of Studley Royal. — 94

16. Henry Steel Thirlway and his wife on the occasion of their 41st wedding anniversary, September 10th 1891. The younger woman standing at the back is probably their daughter, Mary Jane. — 105

Street map of Ripon at the time of the Thirlway journal. — Inside Back Cover

Enlargement of central portion of the street map of Ripon. — Back Cover

FOREWORD

How did the life of the small businessman in Ripon 150 years ago compare with today's equivalent? H.S.T. left a fascinating 10 year record of his life in the city, in a clear but tiny copperplate in a collection of small notebooks.

At the start of his tale the railway had yet to arrive in Ripon, although he made good use of it during its early years. An open millrace still ran the length of Water Skellgate, being the only serious source of power in the city - a far cry from satellite communication, the new town bypass and the power sources of today.

A family man, he was deeply involved in the local civil administration, his church, and a wide range of interests, and he comments on all of these and other aspects of the city's life. In these extracts, edited with great skill by Jean Denton, anyone with any connection with the city of Ripon will find something of interest.

Ripon Historical Society are to be congratulated on sponsoring this publication. Should you wish for more - the original journals are now in the County Record Office at Northallerton - but take a magnifying glass - his writing whilst beautifully legible is incredibly minute.

Rashaad Henry Thirlway
TD, C.Eng. MICE,
30 Finchfield Hill
Wolverhampton
WV3 9EN

ACKNOWLEDGEMENTS

My thanks are first due to members of the Thirlway family: to all those who have so carefully preserved their ancestor's journal, to Mrs Marjorie Heaton née Thirlway who told me of its existence, and most of all to Mr R.H. Thirlway, the diarist's great-grandson, who has not only given permission for these extracts to be published and allowed me to keep the journal in my own home as long as necessary for their selection, but has provided photographs and family details, drawn the reconstruction of Thirlway's Corner shown on the front cover, and, with the permission of Mr Peter J. Adams of Heritage Cartography, has adapted his map of Ripon for use with this publication.

For both local and more general information I have made good use of the ***Ripon Millenary*** and of material in both Ripon and Harrogate public libraries and the library of the University College of Ripon and York St John, Ripon Campus. Amongst those individuals who have provided me with information special thanks are due to Mr Ted Pearson. With regard to illustrations, apart from the family source already mentioned, the portrait of Mrs Lawrence is taken from the ***Ripon Millenary,*** Fossick's drawing of Jepson's Hospital and the picture of Ripon Market Place are from the collection belonging to Ripon Corporation, the railway viaduct photograph has been provided by Yorkshire Image and the St Wilfrid procession in Kirkgate and the two posters are reproduced with the permission of Ripon Museum Trust.

For the support and encouragement they have given to this publication I am greatly indebted to the members of Ripon Historical Society, and especially to Mr John Hebden, Mrs Anna Horsey, Dr W.J. Petchey and Dr John Whitehead for their advice and for the practical help they have in various ways provided. Finally I owe much to Mrs Pauline Litton, who, with the help of Mr John Perkins, has put together the text for the printers, accepting late additions and alterations with cheerful forbearance. Her constructive comments on the presentation of the material have been invaluable.

INTRODUCTION

The journal of Henry Steel Thirlway came to the notice of Ripon Historical Society in 1992 in a letter from one of the society's members, Mrs Marjorie Heaton of California. The society has two sides to its activities, local and family history, and Mrs Heaton (née Thirlway) had joined because her family history researches had revealed a link with Ripon. From the society's quarterly publication, **The Ripon Historian,** she had heard of the Market Place project in progress and realised that the journal in the possession of her English relatives, written as it was by someone who had lived in a Market Place property during the nineteenth century, would be of interest to those engaged in this research and indeed to anyone interested in the history of Ripon. As a result of Mrs Heaton's letter contact was made with the writer's great-grandson, Mr R.H. Thirlway, who readily agreed to send the journal to Ripon and gave permission for extracts to be published. The journal has now been deposited on long term loan with the North Yorkshire County Record Office and has been put on microfilm.

Henry Steel Thirlway (1820-1902) began writing his diary primarily for religious reasons, having read advice from William Cobbett that keeping a diary was a good discipline for a young Christian. His journal therefore includes a large quantity of rather indigestible religious material, but if the reader perseveres he or she will discover many interesting facets of life in early Victorian Ripon. One outstanding contribution is the information provided about the building of the Leeds and Thirsk Railway which ran through Ripon, information he acquired largely through personally inspecting the work during numerous and sometimes lengthy walks in the years 1846-1848. Moreover the writer is revealed as an interesting character in his own right. He emerges from the journal not only as deeply devout and with strong principles, but as physically and intellectually vigorous, with a voracious appetite for knowledge whether acquired from books and lectures or from practical experience and travel. He is also revealed as a man with a deep affection for his family, a love of music and, somewhat unexpectedly because of his other characteristics, a capacity for light-hearted enjoyment. Of course there are a few places where his attitudes jar with the modern reader. He sometimes appears sanctimonious and he was not immune from the prejudices of his class and age, but at least he was prepared to admit to facts that did not entirely fit in with these prejudices. In general he comes over as an attractive personality.

Henry Steel Thirlway's journal was written mainly between 1838 and 1859 although there are fragments made during holidays in 1835 and 1837. However the year 1841 is not covered at all and entries for 1839 and 1840 and for the later years of the 1850s are sparse, so the chief value of the journal is for the year 1838 and the years 1842-1853. Even for the fullest years the entries were not made daily and after 1853 they are notes on the events of the month or even the year rather than being made on the day when things happened. The sparse entries for the period 1839-1841 are accounted for by the writer serving an apprenticeship in York during those years, and those for the later 1850s partly by decreasing leisure time as family, business and public affairs occupied more of his attention, but also by increasing worries about his eyesight which had been troubling him since 1851 at least.

The Thirlway journal is not in a set of uniform volumes. The entries for the 1835 and 1837 holidays and for 1839 and 1840 when the writer was in York are on small pieces of paper subsequently fastened together. Those for 1838 and the years 1842-1859 are in notebooks, some of them apparently bound after the contents had been written, presumably by the writer himself - his York apprenticeship was in bookbinding. These notebooks are also not uniform. That for 1838 is only 3 by 4 inches in size; the remaining ones are about 4 by 7 inches. The notebooks for 1838 and 1846-1850 are paper-backed; those for 1842-1845 and 1851-1859 are hard-backed. Until 1850 each year has a separate notebook; the years 1851-1859 are in the same volume. The journal throughout is written in small but clear handwriting, a sample of which can be seen in Plate No. 3 .

In addition to the journal the 1842-1848 volumes contain what the author calls his "Miscellany" or "Basket of Fragments", mainly consisting of a series of articles on a variety of topics, religious, scientific, literary, local, but with the occasional printed item, for example notices of meetings. The first two of these volumes also contain sets of Bible Class questions and answers. Apart from the volumes already mentioned there are two others in the collection. The first of these is a notebook kept during 1849-1851 to replace the Miscellanies of the earlier volumes. It contains summaries or reviews of books and lectures but the writer soon discontinued these. The second of these additional volumes is a journal kept sporadically by the writer's daughter, Mary Jane, between 1874 and 1880. Some material from this has been included at the end of this book.

For reasons of clarity the extracts in this book have been arranged under headings such as "Family", "Religion" and " Entertainment". For the same reason extra punctuation has been added and capital letters are used in the modern manner. Short explanations have sometimes been added to the text in squared brackets. Longer ones, or further facts concerning the people mentioned in the journal, are to be found in the numbered notes at the end.

1. THE THIRLWAY FAMILY

Although there are a few instances of the name Thirlway (or Thurlow) in the Ripon parish registers of the early eighteenth century the first of these entries known to be connected with the diarist's family is that recording the marriage in 1748 of John Thurlow and Jane Brown, both said to be "of this parish". Both the surname and various indications in the journal suggest that the Thirlways may have originated in north-eastern England and have come to Ripon from Teesside, but no positive proof of this has been discovered. Jane Brown could be the daughter of Roger Brown of Copt Hewick but the name is too ordinary for certainty. In August 1749, the Ripon register records the baptism of our diarist's grandfather, Edward, son of John Thurlow, and in 1773 records Edward's marriage to Mary Teasdale, daughter of William Teasdale. Edward Thirlway (this is the form of the name by which he soon became known) was a barber with his home and business in Kirkgate - the site now occupied by No. 31. Grandfather Edward and Mary were to have eight children altogether, but only five of them survived infancy - four sons and one daughter. Edward's premature death in 1788 shortly after the birth of his daughter, Mary, left his widow with five children to bring up, the oldest being then twelve years of age. Two of the sons, the diarist's uncles, Edward and Thomas, subsequently took up their father's trade of hairdressing. When Uncle Edward died in 1845, the diarist wrote the following appreciation in his Miscellany:

"Mr Thirlway, my uncle, whose death occurred this year was the eldest of the family and has occupied the house and business of my grandfather. My grandfather died when his children were very young. My Uncle Edward was taken from school shortly after and except for a short time at Wakefield and other places for improvement he has followed the same trade, hair dresser, in the same spot ever since. At my grandmother's death who survived her husband a many years and which happened when my father was in London, the property, the house, furniture etc. became my uncle's, but he generously shared it with his sister and three brothers. On the first organisation of the Yorkshire Hussars (1) he joined the regiment (it was during the war with France). They were sent to Scarbro' on duty shortly after. He continued in the regiment for many years.

The trade of my uncle has since his father's death undergone a many change for the worse. Formerly journeymen as well as boys were employed and for three days before a ball they never sat down to meat so busy were they. But the disuse of hair powder took away one half their employment. My uncle then commenced selling toys etc. to fill up the deficiency. But another fashion followed. The wearing of ladies' hair more plain and laying aside of the large tortoise shell combs that were formerly stuck high in the hair. So rapid was this change that my uncle had left on hand several pounds worth and they now remain useless in the shop.

My uncle commenced his illness more than twelve month before its fatal issue, but he only laid some few weeks… He was interred in the family burial ground with his children and by the side of my grandfather and grandmother."

The reference to children in the above passage presumably refers to children who died in infancy, but Edward had three sons who survived him, James, Henry and William. James was a cabinet maker in Leeds when his cousin started his journal. After the death of his parents and his youngest brother he moved back to Ripon and carried on his business in the family home there for many years. The second, Henry, from whom Mrs.Heaton referred to in the introduction is descended, was a mechanic in a steam locomotive works. According to a journal entry for **May 24th 1847**, the works in Manchester where he was then employed had 800 workers and could make 11 locomotives at once. Edward's youngest son, William, followed his father's trade of hairdressing but died unmarried in 1851.

As previously mentioned one other member of the Thirlway family took up the trade of hairdressing. This was the diarist's youngest uncle, Thomas, who moved to Knaresborough and established a business in the High Street there. He was married but is not known to have had any children. The diarist never knew his third uncle, John, who died in 1818 apparently unmarried. His occupation is unknown. The diarist's only aunt, Mary, also never married. She is often referred to in the journal as "my aunt in London". How she came to be in London is unknown although there could be a connection with the time spent in London by the diarist's father. Mary lived in Milbank Street, Westminster where she had a grocery and cheesemonger's business. When she became ill in 1854 the diarist's father went to London, settled her accounts, sold her business and brought her back to Ripon where she lived with her nephew, James, in the family home in Kirkgate for the few weeks before her death.

To turn to the diarist's father, Henry Thirlway. He took up a different trade from his father and brothers being trained as a printer and bookseller, serving an apprenticeship under William Appleton of Darlington, though he may also have spent some of his time in Stockton. An entry in the journal on **Christmas Day 1844,** refers to this period in Henry Thirlway's life.

"..and then came to my ears the sound of bells - the Ripon Minster bells - whose music many, many years ago, as this very morning, fell upon my father's ear when he, tired and spiritless, crossed Hutton Moor, a poor lad tramping from Darlington to see his mother; joy to his heart they brought no doubt which they have never inspired since, even when they have been rung in his honour."

In 1804 some time after completing his apprenticeship Henry Thirlway moved to London. An entry in a deed of 1808 at the time of his mother's death describes him as "Henry Thirlway, bookbinder, of Paternoster Row, City of London". In 1809 he returned to his native Ripon and set up in business in Middle Street. Plate 1 shows what was possibly his first purchase of stock and type from his former master in Darlington. Six years later he married. His bride, Mary Steel, daughter of Matthew and Ann Steel had been brought up after her mother's death by a grandmother and uncle in the village of Grantley to the west of Ripon. Her son describes his mother's arrival in Grantley in an entry made on **September 7th 1845,** when he had been visiting friends in that area:

"...Mr Richmond remembers my mother's first entrance into Grantley. After the death of my grandmother at Dishforth my mother was moved to Grantley and placed under the care of her grandmother and uncle. On the day of her removal

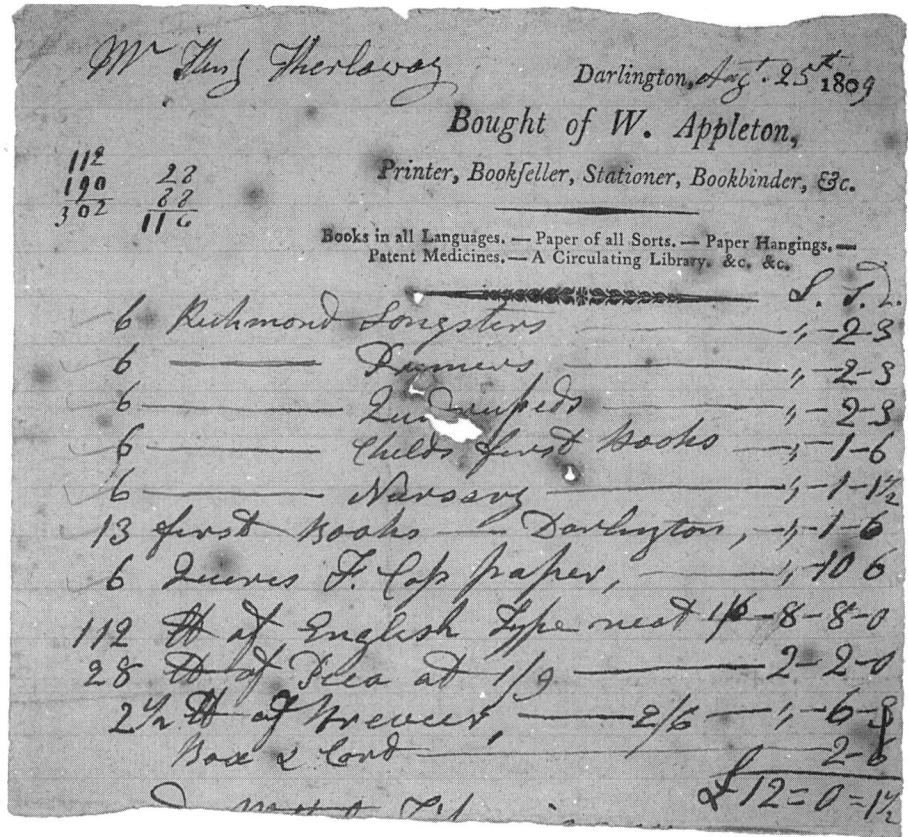

Plate 1. An account believed to be the first order of stock made by Henry Thirlway, the diarist's father, when he set up his business in Middle Street, Ripon, in 1809.

the snow lay very thick on the ground and my mother, quite a babe, was perched upon the top of the cart full of furniture. In passing Low Grantley the road was so obstructed and blocked up with snow that the roads were impassable and they had to go some roundabout road to get to High Grantley, the place of destination. In passing Low Grantley Mrs Richmond's mother took pity upon my mother, brought her into her own house, warmed and fed her and gave her to the present old woman to nurse."

Soon after their marriage Henry and Mary Thirlway moved from Middle Street to the property at the corner of High Skellgate and the Market Place where the business was to remain for over a century thus giving rise to the local name of "Thirlway's Corner". At the time when they moved there (1816) the property was rented from John Britain, local grocer and banker. In 1829 it had to be rebuilt as a result of an early road-widening scheme and three years later Henry Thirlway bought it.

Not long after settling into his new home Henry Thirlway applied to Ripon Corporation for admittance as a freeman. Under a strict application of the local rules, of course, he should have done this before starting his business in the

Plate 2. Jepson's Hospital, the school in Water Skellgate where the diarist received his education.

borough, but at that time the rules were laxly enforced. What made him apply at that particular time can only be a matter for speculation. Pressure from others in the trade now that he had become a more obvious business rival, belief that the Corporation might be looking for a source of funds and it would be wise to move first before being pressurised, desire to take an apprentice, hope for work from the Corporation or even a desire one day to become a member of that body - any one of these or a combination of them must be considered a possibility, the precise timing perhaps being dictated by the expected arrival of his first-born child. The Corporation's response is to be found in the official register.

"**May 19th 1817.** Mr Henry Thirlway, bookseller, a foreigner, applies to take up his freedom of this borough. The three sums nominated and set up by the Mayor are five pounds, ten pounds and fifteen pounds. Whereupon a fine of ten pounds is fixed for the said Henry Thirlway's admission to his freedom. He is admitted and sworn."

The word "foreigner" may seem surprising. Of course this word was used at that time not just for people from outside the country but also of those born outside Ripon, but Henry was a native of Ripon. Probably the term was used because of his apprenticeship elsewhere.

Later that year Mary gave birth to a daughter, christened Mary Ann, and then three years later to a son, our diarist, Henry Steel Thirlway. The little family at Thirlway's Corner was to grow no further. It was a close and affectionate family and the childhood of our diarist seems to have been a very happy one. He was educated at Jepson's Hospital in Water Skellgate where in addition to his charity pupils the Master was allowed to take on a number of fee-paying scholars who according to the journal included "the greater part of the sons of the respectable tradesmen" of Ripon. An extract on John Smith, the schoolmaster from 1827 to 1837, can be found in the section headed "People". Other references to the diarist's childhood concern his playing soldiers on Red Bank to the south of the city where he asserts that his usual role was that of Sergeant-Major though occasionally Major-General and Reviewing Officer, whilst his special school friends, C.J. and T.W. Walbran, brothers of the Ripon antiquary J.R. Walbran, took on the roles of Trumpet-Major and Colonel respectively. Presumably there were some private soldiers for this high-ranking group to command or review! Other childhood experiences in the journal were going cowslipping with his mother and sister, the end product of these expeditions being his mother's cowslip tea and wine - the latter he used to say was better than any port or sherry and to the former he attributed his speedy recovery from an attack of smallpox he had when he was fourteen. Another reference to a childhood expedition is contained in a note in his Miscellany at the time of the death of Mrs Lawrence, the owner of Studley Royal (see "People").

In 1831 and in 1833 he was taken on holidays to the seaside - where exactly he does not record - but it seems likely that it was to the same area which he visited with his father in 1835 just after leaving school. They stayed at Seaton to the north of Teesmouth, a choice probably determined by his father's early connection with that area. It was at Seaton that he made his first attempt at keeping a diary when for a few days he recorded going sea-bathing, watching a yacht race, seeing commercial vessels sailing up and down the Tees and visits to Hartlepool and Sunderland, the latter by sea. Significantly perhaps for the future just about the longest entry concerns the church he attended twice on the Sunday. Returning home he joined his father in the business. Two years later he was taken by his father on his first visit to London where they went to see Aunt Mary and where he was introduced to his father's business acquaintances as well as carrying out an intensive sightseeing programme. On this occasion another attempt at a diary foundered after four days. Commenting on this some time later he wrote that he had intended to write down all that he saw and did on that first visit to the capital "but I soon found by the attempt I made that it was not in my power to perform the task I had set myself. I arose in the morning, breakfasted and we set out on business or pleasure and returned not to our lodgings until night when I was too fatigued to do anything but go to bed". Accounts of later holidays show these to have been equally busy - he became an indefatigable sight-seer - but he had obviously developed greater stamina! (see "Excursions and Holidays").

It was soon after returning from London that he read the book by Cobbett mentioned in the introductory chapter and which led him into keeping a journal in earnest, but having kept it up for a whole year a change in circumstances led to a decrease in entries. His father made arrangements for him to have a three year apprenticeship in bookbinding in York. The plan nearly failed because after the usual month's trial the other employees of Mr George Acton of Petergate pointed out that in taking another apprentice the regulations about the numbers of apprentices allowed to each master would be broken. However, another master, Mr Brassington of Spurriergate, was found and so for three years our diarist was out of Ripon except for brief visits. No doubt conditions during this period were not so propitious for keeping a diary. At any rate entries became sparse with none at all for 1841 and it was only on his return to Ripon in 1842 to rejoin his father that the journal was resumed in earnest. But although his journal suffered, these years in York were to have important consequences for Henry Steel Thirlway's future life.

For the next six years the young man worked for his father in the family business as a journeyman but as he himself records without a regular journeyman's wage, although "all necessaries in diet, clothing, pocket money etc. given me". However, from his account of his activities during this period - entertainments, expeditions, holidays - it is clear that he was not stinted for funds. There was a good relationship between father and son and the latter took an increasingly important role in the business. He had to wait until May 1849, however, before a new sign over the shop read "Thirlway and Son" for the first time.

In the previous year had come a major development in the family with the marriage of the diarist's only sister, Mary Ann, to Richard Parkin of Barnsley. How she had met him is not recorded but his father, Henry Parkin, was a linen yarn agent, and the son is recorded later in the journal as having visited flax spinning mills in Mickley and Nidderdale. The description of Mary Ann's wedding is one of the most delightful passages in the journal.

September 26. My dear sister's thirty-first birthday and her wedding day. The rain had been falling in torrents all night but about eight it ceased to rain. The remaining arrangements were made and a first breakfast got. All were ready punctually at nine when the carriages true to their time arrived. We had two carriages, two greys each, their heads decked with flowers. The postillions had red jackets, gloves, favours etc. The oastler also had a favour and gloves. The bride was dressed in a camelian silk dress thrown out with silver grey, chip bonnet, lace veil and scarf, Honiton lace collar. Orange blossom adorned the breast knot and bonnet. The bridegroom was dressed in black coat and trousers, white satin waistcoat with flowers thrown out. The principal bridesmaids, Misses Parkin and Tuting, wore white silk bonnets and dresses only one shade darker than the bride's - new for the occasion. Misses Hartley and J. Pinn also accompanied the party. The other gentlemen of the party were Mr Thirlway, who gave the bride away, Mr H. S. Thirlway, the groomsman, and Ben Parkin, his (the bridegroom's) brother. We enter the carriages at nine exactly. We took the priest in his course, not wishing to show any favour, to the disappointment of Mr Poole; the canon in residence too, Mr Sutton, would have married them. We were received in the Choir by the Revd J. Jameson who performed the ceremony in a very impressive manner. He took more pains than usual, I was told, pleased I suppose he had not been slighted. The bride and groom went through the ceremony well, speaking out and showing no signs of nervousness. In the galleries and closet pews there were a good number of our friends and others as spectators, more than I expected. On retiring to the Chapter House the sun broke through the clouds and shone in at the old round windows whilst the bells rang out the merry wedding peal. On getting into the carriages my father threw a handful of silver for a scramble. On getting in and out many were the good wishes offered for the happiness of the pair. On returning home our party was augmented by Misses Fisher, Buck and Theakstone. We then sat down to breakfast. The table had been much admired. Thirteen sat down. In the centre sat one of the bride's cakes weighing twenty three pounds; another of similar size etc. was already packed for Barnsley. Round this in profusion, but yet in order, were placed partridges, fowls, tongues, flans, cakes, bread etc., grapes, peaches and nectarines. The whole was beautifully decorated with flowers, the gift of friends. So many flowers were forced in upon us that we had a quantity we could not use at all. Many were the greenhouses and gardens that suffered by their owners that the house and persons of the bridal pair might be gay. After coffee had been served and we had spoilt the look of things in general, we left for the drawing room, the cake and fruit being brought up. In virtue of my office I cut the cake, wine was served and their healths were drunk. At twelve o'clock the couple left us for the station. They had chosen Matlock for their trip which place they reached that night. Misses Tuting and Fisher left us soon after. Thos. Tuting had joined us so the eight that remained had an excursion to Studley in the two carriages we had in the morning with the same postillions etc. ...

On our return from Studley we sat down to a meat tea. As we breakfasted late we had no dinner - we however made up any deficiencies there might be and sorely the poor birds suffered. We then again made our way to the drawing room - more wine and more mirth - for the day was one of pleasure. The party did not break up until about ten o'clock, when we received another and unexpected kindness. The Music Class from the Mechanics Institution serenaded us in the best style they could and well their music sounded as it rose and fell upon the air in the otherwise still street. Thus was spent a day of joy and sadness, of fun and seriousness, of smiles and sobs, kisses and tears, a day on which I received the greatest loss I have ever had. May the Almighty bless them ; may they be blessed on earth and together be for ever in heaven."

Careful readers will have noticed that there is no reference to the bride's mother at the wedding ceremony. Presumably she was at home preparing the magnificent wedding breakfast.

A feeling of loss there might well be. The diarist had never previously known his home without his sister and it was to be three months before he was to see her again. Then he records the great pleasure he felt when Mary Ann and her husband came on a visit for Christmas.

"This Christmas has been looked forward to with great pleasure as it was to bring my sister and her husband and thus bring again all the family together. It has been an happy Christmas for I have seen that my sister is happy with the man she has chosen. My sister brought a branch of mistletoe from Leeds which I have had suspended and under which I had some sweet kisses."

Visits might not be frequent but letters maintained contact and gifts passed between Barnsley and Ripon, hams, cheeses and cakes being the most common although on one occasion Barnsley sent a barrel of oysters to Ripon and Ripon sent a hare to Barnsley. In July 1849, the diarist was most distressed to learn of the death at birth of his sister's first child - a son - and visited her and found her pale and wan, but apparently she made a good recovery and the following year gave birth to a healthy daughter. Her brother was delighted to be asked to act as sponsor at the christening of the new baby.

" **February 18 1851.** Today at eleven o'clock Revd Willan christens my little niece, Mary Thirlway Parkin. Sponsors; - Miss Parkin, Mrs H.S. Thirlway [by this time he himself was married] and myself. At dinner Mr Parkin, Senr., Elizabeth and Ben and ourselves form the christening party. After dinner we drink M.T.P.'s good health and taste her cake, an iced one with her name in full in red and white comfits. After this my wife and I present her with a silver spoon and fork...".

The time has come for the diarist's own marriage to be recorded. Already throughout the 1840s the journal refers to his frequently acting as escorts to ladies to and from church, concerts and balls. On **August 3rd 1847,** for example, he writes "went to concert of Ethiopian Serenaders in the evening. Had the pleasure of seeing four ladies home". In **December 1848,** when he attended the Hussars Ball he wrote, "I was accompanied by the three Misses Buck and Miss Bentham". And on **November 23rd** that same year the diary entry reads, "Martinmas Fair Day. In the evening I took a stroll in the fair with a fair companion, bought her a fairing and as there was a respectable show - a museum in the caravans - we walked into that. I oft visit ladies in their homes and walk them from church, lectures or other public places, but this is certainly an improvement on all that has gone before."

However, when Henry Steel Thirlway married it was not to any Ripon lady but to Miss Alice Ann Mann, elder daughter of a York butcher and farmer. Miss Mann and her father and sister were first pointed out to him when he was walking on the riverside on one of his quite frequent visits to York to visit friends made during his apprenticeship days. It was during the spring of 1849 and soon afterwards he was introduced to her at the home of a mutual friend. On his next visit to York at the end of May that year the Manns invited him to dine with them at their home in the Shambles. His entry for that day ends, "Parted with Alice - may Heaven's richest blessing, a holy, lively faith, be her's, many temporal blessings and more spiritual ones". On a visit in September he reports "11, The Shambles is headquarters now". He stayed there for four days and on the day of his departure writes "Wish goodbye to Alice and hope that the time may come when I can call her my own." Further visits followed during the winter. When he actually proposed to her he doesn't say, but in April the following year his sister visited the Manns and in June Alice Ann accompanied by her younger sister visited Ripon to see "her new home and her new Mama". The wedding was fixed for September 10th that year. Before then Henry Thirlway and his wife prepared to move from Thirlway's Corner to the house next door which they had purchased in the early 1840s. In an entry for **August 31st** our diarist writes "During the week the house next door has undergone various embellishments - a new pot and range set [kitchen range], the staircase papered etc. and during the week father has attended the sales of furniture of Mr Hirst at the Grove and Lacon's at which he has made some purchases." It was at the beginning of that year too that the father handed over the business to his son thus giving him at last financial independence [see "Business" section].

On September 9th our diarist set off for York for his wedding the following day. Let him speak for himself.

"**September 9 :** Up early, get all packed and start by the bus to Boro'bridge a little after seven. One of my companions by the bus was Mr Sayers, formerly landlord of the ***Coach and Horses*** and our neighbour. He has already had three wives and a family by each but not having had sufficient of married life he was on his way to Scarboro' to court 'a ladye faire' - a widow and an innkeeper. I reached York at the usual time and am received at the Shambles by my bride, her sister and cousin Marion, who had come all the way from Ripon to honour the ceremony. [Had he heard of the Misses Mann from this cousin, Marion Ascough, before they were pointed out to him?] And shortly after I am introduced to Aunty Hubbard who has just made a flying visit to York on her way from Scarboro' to her home in Leicester. The first piece of business is the licence procuring. I am accompanied to the Procter's office by Mr J. Mann [the bride's brother] who also accompanies me to Mr I. Grayson, the clergyman of Christchurch [in King's Square, since demolished] and from there to the Clerk's, who I discover to be no other than Billy Grant, the apprentice Mr Brassington had when I was with him. Mr T. Acton accompanies me to order the carriages. In the evening Mr Richard Parkin arrives and the preparations being very busily carried on we get out of the way, make a short ramble about the streets and when we ought to have been going to bed, with the assistance of Mary Ann [the bride's sister] we direct all the cards and write the announcement of our marriage to five newspapers.

September 10 : A nice fair morning but no sun. In the first place the bride must be noticed. Dressed in blue satin with lace mantle, bonnet and veil she looked as lovely as ever bride did. The bridesmaids are Miss Mary Ann Mann, Miss Marion Ascough and Miss Constantia, Miss Ann and Miss Martha, three little nieces of the bride, and Mrs T. Acton. The gentlemen of the party are myself (the bridegroom), Mr J. Mann (who also gives the bride away as Mr Mann did not accompany us to church), Mr W. Mann, Mr T. and J. Acton and Mr R. Parkin. (Mr Ed. Kirby and Mr J. Tuting were both invited but business at Scarboro' detained the one and a sister in Manchester the other). On arriving at the church door we were very politely handed out of the carriage by Mr H. Mills. The ceremony through, the names signed and all made right, we return to the house and soon we set down to a breakfast in beauty and abundance not a whit behind that that sister had. The flowers that composed the bouquets of the ladies and the ornament of the table were the gift of friends. The richest bouquet of greenhouse flowers for the bride were sent from Mr Catton's of Clifton. To the breakfast we had the addition of Mr Mann, Mr Acton and the two Mrs Manns. After breakfast and the usual compliments being paid and the usual cake and wine being put out of sight the happy pair return to their rooms to prepare for the journey. The bride and I are accompanied to the station by Mrs J. Mann and Mr Richard Parkin. Before we leave Yorkshire the sun breaks forth and shines upon my bride …

Not long after our departure from York Mr Lovegrove's carriages are again in the Shambles to convey the party to Castle Howard, where they spent the afternoon, returning to tea at Lobster House.

On the Saturday following, this notice appeared in the papers amongst the marriages:- On the 10th instant, at Christ Church, King's Square, York, by the Revd I. Grayson, Mr Henry Steel Thirlway, Bookseller, Ripon, to Alice Ann, eldest daughter of Mr Mann of the former city." [illustrated on pp10 and 11]

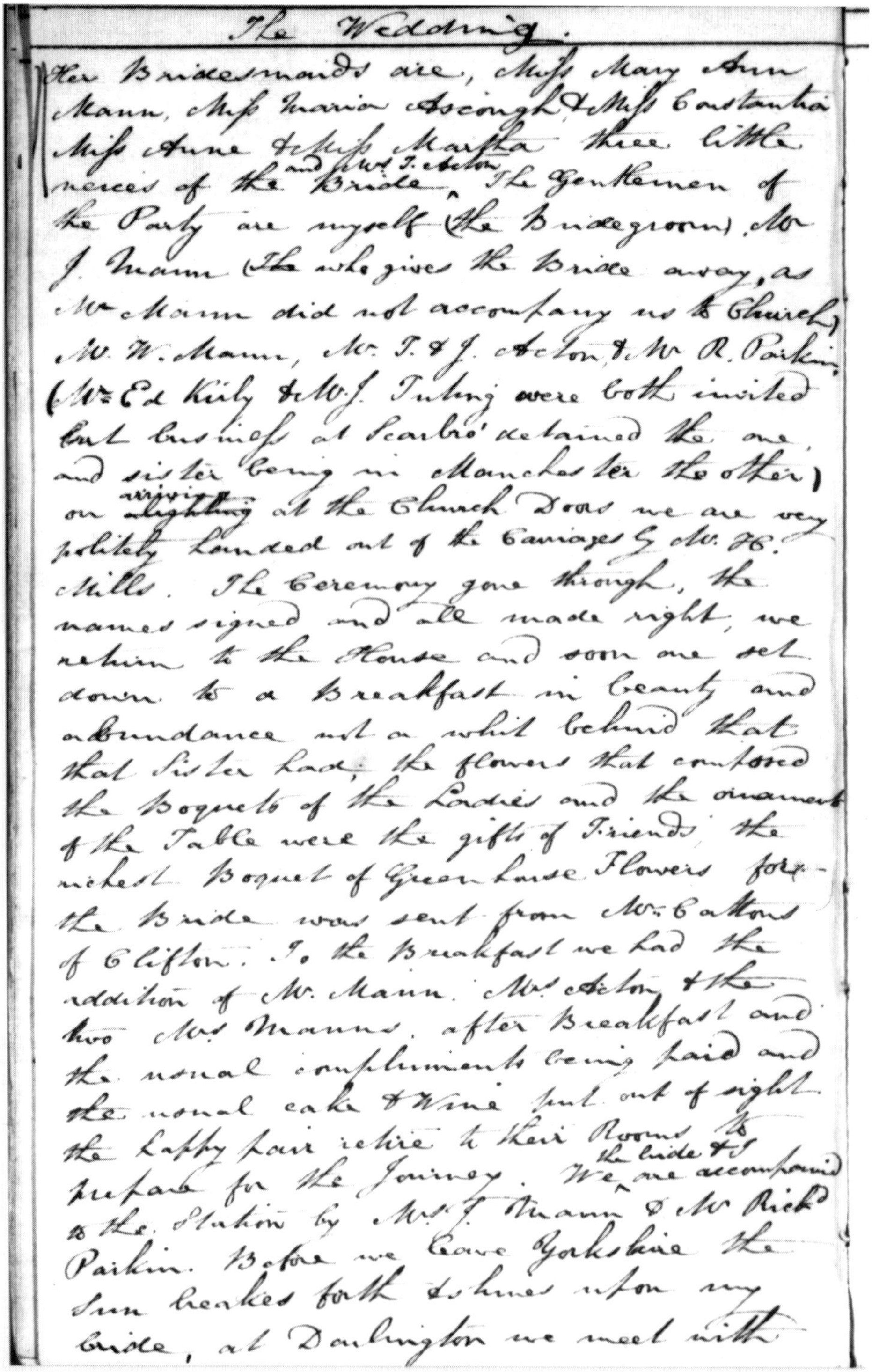

The Wedding.

Her Bridesmaids are, Miss Mary Ann Mann, Miss Maria Ascough & Miss Constantia, Miss Anne & Miss Martha three little nieces of the Bride and Mr & Mrs T. Acton. The Gentlemen of the Party are myself (the Bridegroom), Mr J. Mann (Sen who gives the Bride away, as Mr Mann did not accompany us to Church) Mr W. Mann, Mr T. & J. Acton & Mr R. Parkin (Mr Ed Kirly & Mr J. Tubing were both invited but business at Scarbro' detained the one and sister being in Manchester the other) on arriving at the Church Doors we are very politely handed out of the Carriages by Mr H. Mills. The Ceremony gone through, the names signed and all made right, we return to the House and soon are set down to a Breakfast in beauty and abundance not a whit behind that that Sister had, the flowers that composed the Boquets of the Ladies and the ornament of the Table were the gifts of Friends, the richest Boquet of Green house Flowers for the Bride was sent from Mrs Cattons of Clifton. To the Breakfast we had the addition of Mr Mann, Mrs Acton & the two Mrs Manns, after Breakfast and the usual compliments being paid and the usual cake & wine put out of sight the happy pair retire to their Rooms to prepare for the Journey. We the bride & I are accompanied to the Station by Mr J. Mann & Mr Rich Parkin. Before we leave Yorkshire the Sun breakes forth & shines upon my bride, at Darlington we meet with

Plate 3. Journal open at the account of the diarist's wedding.

The Journey

Rev. R. Poole, at Newcastle we have two hours stay which we devote to seeing a few of the Streets and other objects in Newcastle, we had come across the high level bridge by rail we now walk across it, examine the central station just opened by the Queen, take peeps into the Exchange Room & Market and then take the Rails again, as we shoot along by express Train we now & then get glimpses of the Sea and at Berwick we cross the Tweed by the Royal Border Bridge just named & opened by the Queen. Near eleven p.m. we reach Edinburgh & take a Cab to Sinclair's Temperance Lodgings opposite the Post Office, but the house being full we are directed to Sinclair's other establishment No. 12 South St David Street, Princes Street, to which place our luggage is conveyed. A refreshing Cup of Tea and we soon retire to rest.

Not long after our departure from York, Mr. Lovegrove's Carriages are again in the Shambles to convey the party to Castle Howard, where they spent the afternoon returning to Tea at Lobster House.
On the Saturday following, the following appeared in the papers amongst the marriages. On the 10th inst at Christ Church, Kings Square, by the Rev. I. Grayson, Mr. Henry Steel Thirlway, Bookseller

11

There followed a six day honeymoon in Scotland the account of which can be found in the "Excursions and Holidays" section. It was a very energetic honeymoon full of sightseeing. We can only hope that the bride knew beforehand what she was letting herself in for. Here we resume the story with the account of their return journey to Ripon.

"**September 17** ... At eleven we started from Edinburgh and yet I must linger just to say how favoured we have been. For although it has been misty not a drop of rain has fallen, neither have we had the sun to overpower us. As we fly along by mail train we cannot but admire the country although the hand of autumn rests upon it. At Berwick we are delayed twenty minutes in order to allow the Custom House officers to search for whisky, during which interval we get a good peep at Berwick and the Border bridge. We are hardly over the Border [bridge] before a soldier produces a bottle of whisky, of which out of curiosity I taste. We come through to Thirsk without change of carriage. We are soon on the Leeds and Thirsk line and then soon at Ripon (seven o'clock). On alighting I hear the Cathedral bells ringing merrily. I ask the bus driver what they are going for. He says he does not know. At home we are heartily welcomed by Father and Mother. During the evening a note dated from the Belfry, Ripon, and beginning 'Respected Sir', lets me know why the bells were ringing and at ten o'clock we are serenaded by the Music Class from the Institution [Mechanics Institute]. My Father and Mother for the first time sleep in their new house next door.

September 19 : Today the Revd R. Poole and Revd J. B. Waytes break through all ceremony and come and have wine and cake.

September 21 : Miss M. A. Mann and Mr John Acton arrive this evening to appear at church with us.

September 22 : Our first appearance at church at the Cathedral this morning; an Ordination which we stay to witness. After dinner we walk to Studley Park. In the evening attend Trinity Church ...

September 23 : Mr John Acton returns and Tuesday we sit to receive visitors."

Just about a year later came the first born child of this marriage when Master Henry Mann Thirlway appeared on the scene, an event recorded as follows :

"**September 25 1851** : My wife very poorly...

September 26 : My poor wife worse. Knock up Mr Thos. Gowing (2) and Mary the washerwoman. Nurse and doctor sent for. In the evening our first servant comes to us - had been engaged so as to be a month in the house before the little stranger arrives. Nurse stays all night.

September 28 : Nurse gives her opinion that Mrs Thirlway may go on like this for a month. Poor Alice and Poor Me! The Hussars' band assemble in the Square and proceed to church accompanied by an immense concourse of people. Noon - a change takes place. Doctor Husband fetched in haste. At half-past two o'clock Master Henry Mann Thirlway utters his first cry, a month before he is expected, yet a full grown healthy and fine-limbed child. Grandfather and Grandmother acquainted immediately as well as Uncles and Aunts. The band plays again in the Square. The day closes over a couple of happy, thankful parents. Baby and Mother doing well.

October 14 : My wife and baby get on so well that today nurse leaves us. Her name is Jane Hunter.

October 18 : Baby ill. Doctor sent for. The Revd R. Poole baptises him in the evening. [But a few days later and he is all right again.]

October 26 : Sunday. This morning after Morning Prayers my wife is churched and the baby christened by the Revd R. Poole. Persons present :- Miss Pinn, Mr E. Kirby, Mr H. Mills (Sponsors), Grandpapa and Grandmama, Father and Mother.

In due course two daughters were to follow - Alice Ann in 1853 and Mary Jane in 1858. Sadly Alice Ann was to die in her teens. Mary Jane was to live unmarried until her fifties. Material from her diary kept during the years 1874 to 1880 is to be found in the final section of this book.

After his marriage Henry Steel Thirlway became more involved in public affairs first as trustee to the Municipal Charities and from 1857 to 1860 as an elected member of Ripon Corporation. After two defeats in 1860 and 1865 he does not appear to have sought election again though for many years he continued his work as a Charities Trustee. His son, Henry Mann Thirlway, adopted many of his father's interests. He became prominent in the local church as a lay reader, in the local Volunteer Corps as an expert shot and in local politics first as councillor and then as alderman serving on the Corporation for over forty years. He was Mayor of Ripon on two occasions in 1888-89 and in 1913-14. When he died in 1937 the Thirlway business closed and the Thirlways ceased to live in Ripon. Their premises were purchased by Ripon Corporation and in 1946 were demolished for road improvement purposes. However, many present residents of Ripon still remember the rather dark, cramped little shop at which in their youth they purchased their stationery and writing instruments.

2. THE THIRLWAY BUSINESS

The Thirlway business was never a large one. During the period of the journal it did not employ more than two fully trained men, who for most of the time were the writer and his father, plus two apprentices, although occasional help was given in the shop by the daughter of the family and perhaps by the mother. However, the business, though small, was a varied one comprising that of jobbing printer, bookbinder, stationer, newsagent, bookseller and booklender. The following extracts may seem rather a jumble of disconnected and sometimes not very significant details but it is hoped that cumulatively they will give a good idea of what such a business was like in the early Victorian period.

January 15 1838 : It has been a very hard frost during the night. The ponds are all frozen over. The cistern in the cellar and the water-pot in the printing office were frozen over.

March 24 1838 : In the morning went as is usual to carry newspapers to Revd Charnock's (3).

March 25 1838 : H. Horsefield is at present at home ill in the scarlet fever with which illness several of his father's family have been attacked. Easter, the youngest child, is ill with the typhus fever. G. Horsefield has been sent home ill this evening. [Both Horsefields were Thirlway employees.]

March 28 1838 : Very busy printing and no one but myself and father to do the work.

March 29 1838 : H. Horsefield a great deal better. Came to see us for the first time since his illness. George no better. Procure Geo. a dispensary ticket (4) from Revd Charnock.

April 7 1838 : Henry and George have now returned to their work they having recovered.

May 7 1838 : Cleaned out the printing offices. [This was an annual event.]

May 14 1838 : After tea walked with George to the aqueduct on the River Laver.

June 20 1838 : Went with H. Horsefield to Aldfield Spa (5).

July 14 1838 : H. Horsefield has been off work the whole of this week. His leg is breaking out afresh, leeches having been applied to it and he is now under the care of the dispensary. The breaking out is from an old wound.

July 30 1838 : H. Horsefield returns to work.

November 20 1838 : Received a present of a barrel of oysters from Williams, Coopers, Boyle and Co., our stationers.

December 20 1838 : Richard Hartley came on trial as apprentice.

February 11 1839 : Arrived in York. I came to learn the book-binding business. I came on trial to Mr Geo. Acton, Petergate.

Plate 4. Thirlway's Corner in the late Victorian period. The diarist is standing in the doorway.

March 15 1839 : My father came to York intending to have me bound to Mr Acton, but the journeymen objected to him taking on any more apprentices as he already had got the number allowed by the Binders' Society. The law is that no master shall take more apprentices than journeymen except one for himself.

March 16 1839 : It was agreed that I should stay with Mr Acton a few weeks longer and return home except I should get another situation.

April 8 1839 : Left Mr Acton and went on trial to Mr Brassington, Bookbinder, Spurriergate. Parted with Mr Acton on good terms.

April 20 1839 : Today was engaged to Mr Brassington. I am to stay with him until the end of December 1841.

1840 : Events omitted in their proper places :

In January Henry Horsefield left my father and went to work as a printer at Procter and Vickers (6). H.H. had been with my father upwards of a dozen years (13 years and 3 mths. I think) as an apprentice and journeyman. He got married last year and it may be his wages were too little for him. George Horsefield, his brother, was loose from his apprenticeship this month. He stays on as a journeyman.

January 1842 : Geo. Horsefield, who had served his apprenticeship with my father and worked for two years as journeyman, left us. I having returned from York there is not work to employ both.

In this month my cousin [James Thirlway see 'Family' section] came over from Leeds to make my father a counter, work being slack in Leeds.

March 21 1842 : The new counter was put into the shop.

March 24 1842 : Sold the old one.

May 7 1842 : Today carried home 16 volumes I had been binding for Mr Colling [Mr Collings barrister?]. They were whole bound purple calf, full gilt backs, marble edged.

June 15 1842 : Work very scarce even so that I have little to do for the whole week.

July 25 1842 : This week we have been very busy printing the Missionary Report for last year and the bills for the Anniversary Sermons and Meetings have been among the other jobs we had. Received the engraving of the Minster published by my father (7).

October 7 1842 : Walked up to Fountains Hall after dinner to Revd Joseph Charnock's (3). Our chief object was to visit the Abbey to compare some drawings we have of it with the original … The view fixed upon is from Anne Boleyn's Seat. It has been published thirty years. We are about to have it drawn on steel for a letter-head same as the Ripon Minster sheet which was mentioned before and has given great satisfaction.

October 22 1842 : During the past week we have been very busy printing. The Burgess Roll and the Report of the Society for the Propagation of the Gospel in Foreign Parts are among the jobs we have.

December 22 1842 : This one of the shortest days, yet I saw to print 50 bills at the large press between four and five o'clock in the afternoon.

December 29 1842 : About 7 o'clock one of the barrels of ink in the cellar sprung a leak which was fortunately discovered soon after the mischief begun by Henry and John [Henry Browne and John Shawe - apprentices] who called my father and I to it. The barrel was not emptied until several gallons were on the floor. The greater part was saved by lading it up with tins, saucers, sponges etc. The ink ran from the cellar under the shop down the steps into the pantry, but did no mischief there.

March 14 1843 : About ½ past eight we commenced to set Mr Smith's address (8). We, Henry and I, sat up until ½ past 12 o'clock.

May 1 1843 : Mr Sykes being about to leave Ripon we print for him his bills and a catalogue of twenty pages (9).

August 1 1843 : John Shawe comes into the house to board and lodge according to the indentures.

November 28 1843 : Today I had to finish binding a book containing the marriage service by 11 o'clock (the book I only received yesterday). It was bound in rough calf. I had to recover it, colour it black and letter both on side and back. It was particularly wanted for this morning … there was married in the Cathedral Revd J. W. Hill of Broughton Hall to Maria Frances, only daughter of H. R. Wood Esqr., Hollin Hall.

November 29 1843 : Had another hurried job. Received an order for a book at 5 o'clock last night to be ready by 11 o'clock today. It was lettered "Visitors' Book, St John's National School, Bondgate, Ripon." The book was done on time (10).

December 29 1843 : George Horsefield called upon us and sleeps with us. George was my father's second apprentice. He also worked a time as journeyman. After leaving my father, unable to obtain work at his trade, he abode awhile with his brother at Wadsworth. The brother, Henry, had been my father's first apprentice. As apprentice and journeyman he lived fourteen years with us. Leaving my father he worked above a year at Messrs Procter and Vickers as a printer, when he succeeded in obtaining a situation as schoolmaster and his wife as schoolmistress of the Blyth Boys' National School. Henry took possession of his present situation in the summer of 1841. During last Autumn George has been staying ten weeks in the Central National School, Westminster, where he has been trained as a schoolmaster. George speaks in high terms of the school.

December 30 1843 : George leaves for Skelton where he has friends. George's father and mother for many years lived at the pottery, or rather the brick and tile kilns, near North Bridge. The kiln shades and other buildings were blown down by the great wind, January 1839, and were never rebuilt. In consequence Horsefield moved to Martin Stapylton's at Aldwark near Alne.

January 20 1844 : The nut of the screw belonging to the standing press having given way was replaced today by having four iron pins run through it by Mr Kendall's workmen (11).

March 30 1844 : Mr Browne is interred in the Cathedral burial ground … since his father's death Henry Browne sleeps at home.

June 20 1844 : On June Fair Day John Shawe went home in consequence of his eyes being bad. He is under Dr Earle who orders him to lay in bed, have his eyes bandaged and live low etc.

January 20 1845 : John Shawe goes to Leeds.

February 4 1845 : Shrove Tuesday and being Magazine Day was no holiday for me (12). John being still in Leeds I had to carry out the periodicals.

February 28 1845 : John Shawe has been during the whole month at the Leeds Eye and Ear Infirmary. We have heard little from him. It appears he is no better.

March 12 1845 : John Shawe returns from Leeds no better but with several ointments and drops to apply to his eyes.

April 14 1845 : George Strother, a youth, comes on trial as apprentice.

August 30 1845 : Since Wilfrid [see "Celebrations" Section] my father has had some alterations made in the shop. He had our shelves taken down and the glass case he purchased from our tenant, Mr Blakey, erected in their room.

September 18 1845: Walked over to Boro'bridge to the sale of tools, type, stock etc. of the late Mr Thompson. When we arrived we found the great bulk had been sold by private contract - the type to a young man, the name of Lidell, who is a native of Ripon. He has been apprentice with Walker of Otley and is now going to set up in Heckmondwyke. After father had made a few purchases and called upon our friend, Mrs Carass, and Mitchell, the bookseller, we returned to Ripon.

October 2 1845 : My father returns [from London and Cambridge] ... he purchased the stock, coppers and copyright of **Storer's Delineations of Fountains Abbey.**

October 17 1845 : About five o'clock our kitchen chimney was discovered to be on fire. George had been down to put the glue kettle on the fire. He had put some chips under and then blown some sparks up the chimney with the bellows. It was got out in about an hour and well swept with a machine [a brush?].

October 18 1845 : Today we receive our stock of Storer's **Fountains Abbey** by way of Hull and sell two copies in the evening.

November 2 1845 : Today anthem books have been introduced into the Cathedral. We are the agents for their sale.

November 5 1845 : Today we received the cases for the **Fountains Abbey** and the paper for the titles which we commence printing, when for the first time I saw my name coupled with my father's in print.

November 17 1845 : George Strother was bound apprentice to father and I today.

January 26 1846 : Commenced work at 5 o'clock in the morning to set an address of Hon. Edwin Lascelles to the electors of Ripon (13).

February 2 1846 : Henry Browne's apprenticeship expires today and he takes the following week holiday.

March 14 1846 : Henry Browne who had been working as journeyman for us since the close of his apprenticeship sets out for London this morning.

October 1 1846 : In compliance with a petition from the apprentices of the town the greater part of the shops are to be closed at seven in winter and eight in summer, commencing this evening. Three drapers, Wright, Willey and Durham, are the only ones that refuse (14).

March 24 1847 : Single copies of the Form of Prayer (15) were sent to the clergy and we were desired to print from them to supply the congregations. The type was set from the standard newspaper in consequence of the clergy not having received their copies but on receiving them one was lent us by which we corrected the proof sheet. 900 copies were sold at 1d each, 150 of which were printed after eight o'clock in the evening before the Fast. They were dried, pressed, stitched, cut and above 80 of them were on their way to Aldboro' and Boro'bridge before eight o'clock next morning.

October 16 1847 : During this week we have printed the Form of Prayer and Thanksgiving to be used tomorrow. We first printed 500 copies and today we printed 500 more - all of which were sold.

March 2 1848 : Had a quick trip of two miles on the Leeds road. A couple, man and woman, had been in Ripon some few weeks selling trunks, but finding trade bad they this morning decamped, putting the key of the furnished house they had lived in under the door, leaving a debt of six shillings at a small shop and taking a full set of novels belonging to our library. The young man who keeps the shop, when he found they were gone, came to me. He dare not follow them unless someone would go with him, so we started and overtook them opposite Hood Hole. I regained the 1st volume of the set only. The shopkeeper got nothing, for the poor fugitives had nothing or would confess to nothing.

April 29 1848 : Ordered a printing press of Messrs Clymer, Dixon and Co.

May 12 1848 : Took the old printing press to pieces. It was an old one when my father bought it of Mr Bell of Richmond in the year 1829.

May 13 1848 : Arranged the printing office as the compositors' room, clearing the old compositors' room for the new press.

May 18 1848 : The new printing press arrives at the station, it having come by Goole and York by water and then per rail.

May 19 1848 : Had the floor of the press room over the staircase strengthened.

May 20 1848 : The press arrived a little after nine. The staple weighing about half a ton was considered a difficult thing to carry up stairs so a derrick and four guy ropes were erected on the top of the staircase, to which pulleys were attached, and part of the hand rail being taken down it was drawn up. The arrangements were under the direction of Thomas Gowing (2). In all we had about eight men to assist in this job which, being attended with danger to the house and the men employed, made us feel afraid. In the afternoon the press was put up.

May 27 1848 : The revolution in the printing office is now complete. The new press has been worked and answers well. The painters etc. very busy on the staircase.

August 1 1848 : Today John Shawe's apprenticeship expires.

August 2 1848 : John gets his indentures and proceeds home as we are not very busy.

September 18 1848 : John Shawe leaves Ripon for London.

October 30 1848 : Charles Ingram comes on trial as apprentice for a month.

November 27 1848 : His month being completed Charles' father and mine made an agreement that he should serve two years for nothing, three for six shillings a week, and two for seven. When I became aware of this I objected and Mr Ingram called again. I told him I should be paymaster and I could not think of paying so much more than other people. I offered him seven shillings a week for the last four years but, at my father's request, I offered five shillings for the third year, six for the fourth, fifth and sixth, and seven shillings for the seventh. This did not please Mr Ingram and he kept Charles away for a day. At length it was agreed that he should come at the last named terms - which are higher than ought to be given - two years no wage, one year five shillings, three years six shillings, one year seven.

January 13 1849 : Most of the bills have come in that are against us, and I have had the pleasure of paying the majority of them. [Another annual event.]

February 20 1849: Shrove Tuesday. The great half-day holiday for apprentices. The day was very fine and numbers flocked to Red Bank [to the south-west of Ripon] and other fields to play at spell and knor and cricket.

March 27 1849 : Charles Ingram bound to us by Mr R. Robinson [solicitor of Bedern Bank]; his apprenticeship commenced November 27 1848.

May 21 1849 : Today was reared over our shop front a new sign which (for the first time) displays the words "Thirlway and Son".

January 1 1850 : During the past month my father has been taking stock. He values the stock, presses etc. at £350 all of which he gives me, and this morning I commence business on my own account. Since my return from York I have had no wage or salary but all necessaries in diet, clothing, pocket money etc. given me.

June 10 1850 : After going to bed and almost to sleep I am knocked up by Gas Matthew to make out a bill for gas consumed by Gigliardi's [Circus] who are pulling down to go away. This done I get to bed again and before I can tumble over to sleep I have to get out of bed again to see where the great light and noise proceed from. And find that Gigliardi's are no niggards at burning gas after the meter has been taken [read]. Twelve lights at full blaze are burning away to give them light to pull their show to pieces and pack up.

September 2, 3, 4 1850 : The greater part of these days have been busy cataloguing and labelling for the library of Digby Cayley Esqr. (16), with George, my apprentice, for an assistant. The library contains more than 2,000 volumes and is a collection of sermons, divinity, classics, travels, fictions etc. It was collected by "Parsons Allanson", the father and grandfather of Mrs Cayley.

January 20 1851 : Today commenced a banking account with Messrs Terry and Harrison's (17) by depositing with them £50.

March 31 1851 : [H.S.T. copies out his entry on the census form. This includes G. Strother, apprentice, unmarried, male, 19, printer and bookseller, born Ripon.]

April 1 1851 : For the last few years all the principal shops have been closed at seven o'clock for six months commencing with October and at eight commencing with April for the other six months. Today, however, I am waited upon by Messrs Harrison, Judson and Fairburn (18) requesting me to agree to close for the month of April at seven, which I agree to, and the treaty is ratified by our having a glass of bitter each, for which it falls to the lot of Mr Harrison to pay.

April 1851 : During this month John Shawe returns from London and commences business at Masham.

April 26 1852 : George is loose from his apprenticeship and has a tea party. I go and have a glass with them.

June 14 1852 : Today Richard Taylor is bound to me as a printer and bookbinder from the 26th of February, the day he came, until the 7th of May 1858 (his 21st birthday). The particulars of the indenture are :- two years no wage, third year four shillings per week, fourth and fifth years five shillings per week, sixth and to the end of the apprenticeship six shillings per week. It is usual to have a month on time with apprentices but Richard had been many weeks with Mr Harrison from whom he had been removed in consequence of their unwillingness to learn him bookbinding. So that Richard came to me with a good stock of knowledge and was useful at once. A good deal of arguing and countering had to be gone through before the terms could be adjusted, Mrs Taylor in place of her husband being rather hard at a bargain.

August 1852 : During this month George Strother leaves and in a week or two gets a situation at Rother[h]am.

September 25 1852 : Father still from home [visiting Mary Ann at Barnsley] and I very busy. Our chief job is the Ripon Bazaar Gazette, 4 pages of 3 columns each demy 4. In the midst of our throng H. Horsefield, an old apprentice of my father's, comes from Boro'bridge and offers his assistance which I accept.

March 1855 : Richard Taylor, my youngest apprentice and who had been with me since February 1852, being likely to leave me, I look out for another apprentice. His mother, who keeps a wine and spirit vault in Westgate, and his eldest brother, a grocer's shop, along with the whole family are about to emigrate to America. The Taylors were booksellers at Bedale. The old man has died since their removal to Ripon. They possess property at Galpha[y] and other places. I have an errand boy for a week but he would not like to be an apprentice. (Henry Groves, the youth in question, afterwards goes to be a pupil teacher at Trinity Church schools.)

April 2 1855 : William Rudd comes on trial as an apprentice. Richard still continues with me. His brother sells off his stock of groceries etc.

May 12 1855 : Richard Taylor leaves me with my full consent but the indenture remains with Mr Robson [Robinson?]. William Rudd is bound to me from the 1st of May 1855. First year no wage, second and third year 3/- per week, fourth year 4/-, fifth year 5/-, sixth year 6/-, seventh year 7/-.

September 18 1855 : A general illumination and rejoicing for the fall of Sebastopol. We made for several people transparencies, crowns, mottoes, etc. The townspeople display much taste.

November 1855 : Charles Ingram's apprenticeship expires on the 27th.

February 1856 : Work being slack Charles Ingram, my journeyman, leaves me and is employed by Mr Judson (18).

In **September** I am appointed Distributor of Stamps (19).

October 2 1856 : Receive the first consignment of postage stamps.

October 11 1856 : Received the stock of skins (20) etc. from Mr Judson the late stamp distributor. Mr W. Judson had held the office since it was vacated by Mr W. Harrison (18 and 21) in 1855.

1857 : During the last two months of the bygone year and the first six weeks of the present Charles Ingram is again at work in the office. He then proceeds to London but returns out of health and in October is again at work for me and continues with me.

1859 : During the first half of the year Charles Ingram works for me. At midsummer he leaves for the purpose of entering the service of the N.E. Railway Company.

3. RELIGION

Henry Steel Thirlway and his family were devout Anglicans. As indicated in the introduction to this book the main reason for starting the journal was a religious one and so religious matters play an important part in it, far more than any other topic. The following extracts therefore are only a small sample of the many entries dealing with church matters and the religious life of the writer.

1838 [this is the first entry in the journal] : Send down thy Holy Spirit upon me O Lord that whatsoever I write in this my journal now commenced may lead to the advancement of true religion in me.
[Series of dots in the next few extracts indicate where summaries of sermons have been omitted.]

January 7 1838 : An Ordination was held by the Bishop (22) in the Cathedral. The Very Revd the Dean (23) preached the ordination sermon. 11 priests and 12 deacons were ordained. Revd R. Poole (24) preached in the evening … In the afternoon one of the priests who had been ordained in the morning preached at Trinity Church. Revd Shadwick preached in the evening.

March 25 1838 : Attended Sunday School. The Lord Bishop of Ripon preached in the morning from the 66th Psalm, 18th verse, 'If I regard iniquity in my heart, the Lord will not hear me' from which he made a very eloquent and impressive sermon. In the afternoon the Very Revd the Dean delivered a very beautiful and impressive sermon from the 37th chapter of Genesis 1st verse 'And Jacob dwelt in the land wherein his father was a stranger' … Attended Trinity Church in the evening. Revd J. W. Whiteside (25) preached an excellent sermon. His discourse was on uncharitableness from which sin deliver me Lord.

August 19 1838 : Wilfrid Sunday (26). Attended Sunday School and Minster in the morning. The Very Revd the Dean preached from the 22nd Chapter of the 1st Book of Kings, 8th verse …

Attended Minster again in the afternoon. The Dean preached from the 17th Chapter of Acts, 31st verse …

Attended Trinity Church at night. Revd W. Plues (27) preached from the 2nd of Hebrews, 3rd verse …

Great wickedness has this day gone forward. Early in the morning the race horses were practising on the course, the ballad singers were selling lists of the races, and people were drinking in the tents all day.

August 26 1838 : Sunday. Set out at 7 o'clock this morning along with my father, mother and sister in a car to Dacre Banks. We arrived in time to go to church. The church is a new one and was built by subscription in 1837. It contains 400 sittings, 300 of which are free. After dinner we took a walk to Dacre and returned in time to go to church. After tea we set out again and gained home at after eight. [The Thirlways had an elderly relation in Dacre.]

Plate 5. The Right Reverend Charles Thomas Longley, D.D., first Bishop of Ripon.

August 28,29,30 1838 : A bazaar was held in the Town's Hall or more properly Mrs Lawrence's Hall, Market Place (28), for the purpose of raising a fund of which two-thirds are to be applied for building a parsonage house at Dacre and one-third for the National Schools in Ripon [Church of England day schools]. The sale of articles at Ripon Bazaar amounted to £350 or near it. A many articles are yet unsold.

September 28 1838 : Went to a meeting held in Trinity Church school room of the London Society for Promoting Christianity among the Jews. The Bishop presided ...

September 29 1838 : Attended a meeting in Mrs Lawrence's Hall, Market Place - the first public meeting of the Society for the Propagation of the Gospel in Foreign Parts. The Bishop in the chair ... Collection £50/2/6.

October 1 1838 : The day was beautiful and fine and the adjoining ground was crowded with carriages of every description but there were not as many of the lower orders as might have been expected when the Bishop drew up to lay the first stone of the Episcopal Palace on Ripon Parks (29). The Bishop offered up prayer and then went through the usual ceremony of laying the stone. [Various speeches followed.] The Mayor and Corporation, the Police, the Dean and Chapter and the Gentlemen and Magistrates preceded by the Hussars' Band attended the ceremony in procession ...
A lunch was provided by the Bishop at his residence to which the gentry etc. were invited. The workmen employed were regaled with roast beef etc. for supper which was served up in the Riding School (30).

October 23 1838 : The Sunday and National School boys were treated today in the Girls' National School Room St.Agnesgate] with tea and cake, and last Friday the girls were treated in the same manner. The room was decorated with festoons of laurel, flowers etc.

1839-1842 The writer served an apprenticeship in York.]

August 16 1840 : Wilfrid Sunday. Set out with Thos Acton for Ripon. We set out early in the morning with Mr Bingley, Butcher, Petergate in his car. O Lord forgive Thine unworthy servant this sin and grant that for the time to come he may by Thy grace successfully resist all temptation which may beset him of Sabbath breaking.

1842 : [Three months after his return from York H.S.T. resumed his journal with a mention of a number of recent events.]

January 1842 : I frequently visited the National (Boys) School on the Sunday in consequence of the Sunday School being removed there (10). Mr Bickers having given up being Master, Mr Hewitson, National School Master, took it. The boys are taught by monitors on the National system. After a little delay succeeded in getting a class. I am the only voluntary teacher.
On Christmas Day Revd W. Gray (31) acted for the first time as Canon in Residence. He stayed at the Residence for three months. He was succeeded by the Revd P. W. Worsley (32). Mr Gray was the first canon who did this duty, as there was no residentiary canon before. but according to the present alterations one of the canons will always be at Ripon. A very good law.

25

March 13 1842 : Being engaged today for the first time I attended Littlethorpe Sunday School. The school was formed by Misses Maister (33) and since their departure for Barbadoes Miss Serjeantson formerly of Camphill having the house conducted the school, but as they have gone into the south for the winter Misses Gray have attended to it. They having left with their father, I have undertaken to supply the place until Miss S's return which will be in May.

April 12 1842 : Went to Wesleyan Methodist Chapel [on Coltsgate Hill] to hear the Anniversary Sermon expecting to hear Mr Rattenbury of York but Mr Roebuck of York preached instead.

May 16 1842 : In the afternoon the children as is usual on Whit Monday walked in procession from Skellgate Chapel to the one in Priest Lane (34).

June 13 1842 : Attended a Teetotal meeting. Job Marchant, preacher of the New Connexion, was the chief speaker. Henry Browne, my father's apprentice, signed the pledge [i.e. to abstain from alcohol].

June 19 1842 : Mr Hewitson being from home I had the care of the National School boys. Anything but a pleasant task.

November 3 1842 : This week the workmen are busy taking down the scaffolding in front of the Minster after having repaired the top part of the gable and added a cross on the top. Many people object to crosses on churches and nickname it Puseyism (35). I can see no objection to them so long as we give them no veneration. When we are admitted into the Church of Christ we are signed with the sign of the cross, nor should we, I think, ever be ashamed of it, so long as we put no trust in these things but trust in Christ and Him alone.

November 27 1842 : In the evening I attend the New Connexion of Methodists' Meeting House and hear Job Marchant preach; his discourse was from the beginning to end levelled against the Socinians (36).

April 13 1843 : In the evening a meeting was held in the Public Rooms for the purpose of opposing Sir James Graham's National Education Bill. I did not attend, but have been told that the speakers ran away from the real question and abused the Tory party most unmercifully. Job Marchant denounced the clergy of the Church of England as drunken parsons and the people as willing to believe the Koran as the Bible. People and clergy altogether men who would like to cut off people's ears that did not agree with them. [See April 28 entry for more on this topic.]

April 18 1843 : Easter Day. My father accompanied by his family received Sacrament at the Cathedral at 7 am. Today for the first time we sit in the Choir, intending to give up our old pew, seat No. 12 in the North Gallery, which we have occupied for about 28 years. Our new seat is No. 22. [After this he discontinued taking notes during the sermons.]

April 28 1843 : Lately I recorded a meeting on the subject of education held by Dissenters. I now record with more pleasure a lecture on the same subject. It is relating to the Factory's Bill for the formation of schools. The lecture took place in Trinity Church School by the Revd Mr Whiteside. He showed from Parliamentary reports the awful degradation of many thousands who live in the manufacturing

Plate 6. Ripon Minster as shown on Thirlway notepaper mentioned in the journal.

towns and the vices into which they had fallen and the ignorance which prevailed. He drew attention to the errors which prevailed to the bill being intolerant, which it is not, as it provides that no one shall be obliged to learn Church Catechism or anything else if the parent has religious scruples. My most earnest wish is that the bill may pass. Our Bishop lately in a conversation with my father said he believed that nothing had been introduced into Parliament so beneficial to the country since the Reform Bill.

August 11 1843 : The Bishop held a Confirmation in the Cathedral when about 450 young people were confirmed. Henry Browne and John Shawe, our apprentices, were of the number.

October 29 1843 : At the National School great changes are about to take place. Mr Giles from the Central National Society School, London, has come into the diocese on order to reorganise the schools (37). I was introduced to him this morning.

November 5 1843 : All the old desks in the National School are cleared away - this morning I taught the second class from (Marick's ?) Catechism - everything in the school on a new plan. Today being the anniversary of the memorable and infamous Gunpowder Treason and the day when William III landed in England the service appointed for that day was read in the Cathedral and Trinity Church.

April 11 1844 : Sir John Barleycorn [strong drink] was tried before a Judge and Jury yesterday evening in the Temperance Hall before a crowded audience. Tonight it is to be repeated by particular desire.

February 14 1847 : Today the Bishop preached in obedience to a Queen's letter for the suffering Irish and Scotch. Amount collected £16. The amount collected amongst the inhabitants before the Queen's letter was made known was near £400.

April 24 1847 : Today a General Fast is kept through England, Ireland and Scotland in consequence of the famine which prevails in Ireland and some parts of Scotland. The Fast was called by a proclamation from the Queen.

May 9 1847 : This evening we sit in pew No. 64 at Trinity Church for the first time having left our old pew No.154 in which we have sat during the last twenty years. Reasons for giving up the pew are its being near the window is cold and dirty, we have the whole pew four sittings, only two of the family attend at once so we take half of a better pew, Mr Thwaites having the other half (38).

December 17 1847 : The Hon. and Revd D. Erskine was duly installed Dean of Ripon today. [Dean 1847-1859; buried in Cathedral graveyard.] The canons present were Worsley, Sutton and Gray.

February 6 1848 : Some alterations having taken place in the National School, I am induced to teach the first class instead of the second class. Today the Dean reads himself in and preaches twice.

February 20 1848 : The Dean preached in the Cathedral this morning. He also preached last Sunday afternoon. He has already made some few alterations in the church. For one thing he has had removed from the altar the two candles and brass dishes which for long have ornamented it according to the usage and canons of the Church.

March 20 1849 : Today the Bishop lays the first stone of the Parsonage House to Trinity Church in the presence of a concourse of people. In the stone was inserted a glass bottle containing a list of the contributors' names. Over this was placed a brass plate on which is engraved a suitable inscription. The Bishop gave a very suitable address - Revd W. Lewis offered up a prayer. The 100th Psalm and the National Anthem were sung.

September 26 1849 : Day of Humiliation and Prayer [because of the outbreak of cholera] has been fixed for today. A notice signed by the Mayor has been published recommending that the shops should be closed from 8 to 1 and from 6 o'clock for the rest of the day, but the great majority were never open at all. The churches and chapels were well attended.

March 23 1851 : Sunday. Mr Gray who has been three months in residence preaches his last sermon today. The first part at the Cathedral morning service and the second part of it in St John's in the evening. Having heard the former half of the discourse we go to St John's in the evening, and after that I walk up to Trinity Church which is lit up tonight with gas for the first time.

1857 : On the 8th of May our newly elected Bishop (Dr Bickersteth) preaches his first sermon in Ripon Cathedral (39).

During the same month the Revd Thos Tuting pays his farewell visit to Ripon prior to his embarkation for India as a missionary.

4. THE MECHANICS INSTITUTE

Next to the Church the institution in which his Journal shows Henry Thirlway to have been most interested was the Ripon Mechanics Institute and Literary Society to which he often referred simply as "the Institution." It was founded in 1831, one of a chain of such Institutes across the country which were designed to provide facilities for self-improvement for wage-earning men, especially the skilled artisan. To it was joined in 1844 a Literary Society which in a larger town would probably have been a separate organisation with a larger percentage of members from the more educated, cultured classes. When the twentieth century provided opportunities for secondary education and even college or university for intelligent children of the working classes, the Mechanics Institutes began to decline. That in Ripon ended in 1927 and its by then largely social function was taken over by the newly formed Ripon Citizens' Social Club (now the Ripon City Club). The following extracts give some indication of the activities of the Mechanics Institute in its youthful heyday, and of the part played in them by Thirlway himself.

7 April 1844 : In the evening received my card as member of the Mechanics Institute and Literary Society. My father had lately become a member but has transferred his membership to me.

16 April 1844 : Attended the Institution and joined the Drawing Class under H.W. Todd.

15,16,17 October 1844 : Three public Conversations and Promenade Concerts took place in connection with the Mechanics Institution and Literary Society in the Public Rooms (40), the whole of which were occupied and fit[ted] up in a very pretty style. Over the door, in coloured lamps, was displayed a regal crown with the letters V. and A. The staircase was arched over and covered on each side with laurel which gave it the appearance of a winding path in a bower or wood. This was also illuminated with lamps. In the large room was erected an orchestra in the form of a Grecian terrace, above which the arms of Ripon, the Royal Standard and the Union Jack were painted with the motto "We labour in hope." At the opposite end, and in strict keeping with the orchestra, was erected a very neat screen which stretched across the breadth of the room and was divided into three compartments by pillars. The centre was the entrance to the room; those on each side were fitted with counters where tea and coffee were served by ladies who stood behind them. On the top of this screen excellent full length casts of the Queen, the Prince etc. were placed. Along the screen ran the words "Amusement with study in Mechanics Institutions." The walls were covered with pictures kindly lent for the purpose. A catalogue of these would be too long yet I may mention two portraits, one of Mr. Elliott of India, brother to Misses Elliott of Ripon [see "People" section], the other that of S. Tutin in his robes as Mayor of Ripon. A moonlight landscape and the head of a brigand attracted a good deal of attention.

In the small room a French cottage was erected where those who wanted something stronger than tea or coffee could have their wants supplied by paying for it - the wine and spirits being sold in it. To the left another room was neatly set out with supper, where for a shilling extra a good tuck out might be obtained.

The admittance was but a shilling each evening. On the first night a few short of 500 was present. The meeting was opened at seven o'clock by speeches from Dr Earle (the President), W. Williamson and Mr Norman who gave us an history of the Institution from its commencement ... At eight o'clock tea was served and at nine o'clock the Amateur Musical Society assisted by Julian Adams and Herr Kohler commenced the concert which continued until near 11 o'clock.

The band was full and effective. "Fra Diavolo" and "Cenerentola" were admirably played, also the pianoforte and flageolet. The songs "Britain's Home" and "O Albion" were well sung. John Adams gave also two solos on the pianoforte and Herr Kohler a solo on the cornet à piston which were much admired.

On the second night the rooms were more crowded than on the first. Mr. Cameron, the leading man in the Wakefield Institution, gave an address on the benefits of Mechanics Institutions. At eight tea was served and shortly after the Hussar band in uniform occupied the orchestra and played several martial airs and the polkas; at intervals Messrs Womersley, Gott and Hussey sang several glees and songs. ... On the third night the room was not so crowded, although it was well filled ... at nine o'clock Mr Huggins, of Leeds, gave an highly interesting lecture on chemistry, illustrated by many experiments. ...

The designs for the orchestra etc. were made gratuitously by Mr Todd who superintended their erection. Mr Darnton, Mr Burton, painters, Mr Brown, the artist, and the workmen of Mr Norman also gave much time and labour.

3 November 1844 : Monthly meeting at the Institution. 22 new members are elected, after which a discussion takes place on hiring a house or building rooms for the purpose of the Institution, the present room being inadequate to our wants.

26 November 1844 : Special meeting at the Institution for the purpose of considering the expediency of building our hall for ourselves or building a room on other peoples' property at the end of the Public Rooms - conclusion, nothing settled - meeting adjourned.

3 December 1844 : Annual meeting at which Mr Blakey and Mr Norman quarrel. Mr B. full of satire, Mr N. full of rage. [J. Norman, carver, gilder, upholsterer]

13 December 1844 : Dr Murray commenced a course of seven lectures on Chemistry in connection with the Institution. The first delivered tonight was on Poisons ...

16 December 1844 : The second lecture on Fermentation etc.

18, 19 December 1844 : Lectures on Agricultural Chemistry. Very few farmers attend.

20 December 1844 : Sixth Lecture. The Eye and the Nature of Vision and the Ear.

23 December 1844 : Last. Subject: the Diamond.

7 January 1845 : A meeting at the Institution agreed that the newspapers be sold after they have remained a time in the room.

21 January 1845 : Attended the Mechanics Institution for the purpose of drawing. Since Mr Todd's departure the Drawing Class has fallen away. Glaves [?] and I are the only remaining members. Some have entirely given it up, others have commenced drawing plans of houses etc. whilst others draw figures, landscapes etc. which are more easy and more viewly than diagrams.

23 January 1845 : Mr Thomas read a paper on contagious diseases at the Institution.

3 November 1845 : Today **Hamlet** is read by Mr C. Kemble. The Mechanics and Literary Institution have engaged him for two nights, on the first to read **Hamlet** on the second **Much Ado About Nothing,** for which he is to receive £40. Tonight the room was well filled. The reading was very good and appeared to give satisfaction.

21 February 1846 : Attended a lecture on Geometry by Mr Thurnell in connection with the Institution. Mr Thurnell I do not doubt is very clever in Geometry but he is not an attractive lecturer. Nevertheless his lecture to me was highly instructive. He showed how Geometry was applied to the Arts, Sciences and Manufactures, especially to Astronomy. He also described that useful article the sextant. The lecture was illustrated by diagrams.

3 March 1846 : The first monthly meeting is held when a lecturer is engaged to give lectures on "Elocution" in June next.

18 June 1846 : Mr C.J. Walbran (41) gives a lecture on Shakespeare's **Macbeth** in connection with the Institution.

26 February 1847 : The Annual Meeting ... Officers elected as usual and the question as to whether a new building should be erected for the Institution or not. The business, however, which caused most interest was the election of a school master. Since Mr Bishop left the town, Mr Dixon, schoolmaster at Trinity Schools, has had the management. The candidates for the office were four :- Mr Dixon, Mr Gardener, a shoemaker, Mr H. Bell, a washerwoman's husband, and Mr Rowe, schoolmaster formerly of Galpha[y] now resident at Sharow. The election was open for all 1st and 2nd class members to vote. The issue was - Mr Dixon 48, Mr Bell 19, Mr Gardener 5, Mr Rowe -.

7 April 1847 : a monthly meeting of the Institution when several new members were elected, the newspapers sold and the project for a new building was further gone into. A plan was laid before the meeting for building a new "hall" at the end of the Public Rooms and a resolution was passed empowering the committee to purchase the necessary ground for £150. It is estimated that £1,000 will be required to complete the whole. £90 was subscribed by the members then present.

After the **7 April 1847** entry Henry Thirlway inserted an advertisement of two lectures to be given in the Institute:

5 May 1847 J.H. Hudson, "History of Novels and Comic Romances"

6 May 1847 Mrs Hudson, "The Lives and Genius of Distinguished English-women".

H.S. Thirlway's comments:
The first of these lectures was but poorly attended although free, in consequence

of the shortness of the notice. Mr Hudson is Secretary to the Yorkshire Union of Institutes and resides at Leeds. The lecture was entertaining and showed that comic writings are not without their use. Satire will sometimes mend a man of a fault when all other reproofs have failed. In concluding he wished to observe that fiction, novels etc. were only allowable so far as they did not interfere with other duties and studies.

Mrs Hudson's lecture was well attended. The subject was well handled. It was recounting the works and doings of literary ladies from the earliest to the present time. Woman as a writer I like, also woman as a companion, but woman as a public lecturer looks like woman out of her place (42).

6 March 1848 : Annual Meeting ... I am elected on the Committee. A few weeks ago I was made a trustee for the new building.

13 May 1848 : Elected Treasurer and Secretary of Music Classes.

27 October 1848 : This evening I together with several more trustees sign the covenant and conveyance deeds for the Mechanics Hall (43).

31 October 1848 : At a special committee meeting the check [sic] was made out for the £150 for the purchase money to be paid by the Ripon Mechanics Institution to the Proprietors of the Public Rooms for the land to build on.

15 December 1848 : This evening a committee meeting is held at which the contracts are let for the building of the hall.

20 December 1848 : Today the foundation stone of the Mechanics Hall was laid by W. Williamson Esq. (44). In the stone was inserted a bottle containing a **Leeds Intelligencer** and the names of the Committee.

25 January 1849 : Tonight there was a public evening of rather a novel kind at the Institution, got up not by the heads of the Society but by the working men. It was commenced by a short lecture on "Elocution" by C.J. Walbran. This was followed by an overture performed by the Music Class (their first appearance). Then a presentation. Then followed a set of quadrilles. Waltzes were then played and the evening's entertainment concluded with "God Save the Queen". The band consisted of those members of the class who were good players - it was composed of 5 violins, 1 violincello and 6 flutes. I did not intend to appear but I yielded to persuasion in consequence of the small number of violins that were up to the mark.

21 February 1849 : During the present winter we have a weekly lecture at the Institution by gratuitous lecturers. This evening however was an extra night. Professor Partington was engaged to lecture on "The Electric Telegraph and Electric Light." The room was crowded, 108 reserved seats were taken. The Professor was to receive £3 for his services but he gave it up, requiring only his expenses. The receipts of the evening were to be added to the building fund. Mr P. explained the old systems of telegraphing and then the new mode of electricity. He also made some short observations on the electric light, which he condemns strongly.

19 April 1849 : The first meeting in the new hall for the Institute. Am placed on the managing committee for making the arrangements for opening the new building with a dinner etc.

1 May 1849 : Practised with the Music Class for the first time in the new school room.

22 May 1849 : Today the new hall for the Mechanics Institute and Literary Society is opened by a public dinner. 65 persons sat down to dine. The Dean in the chair, the vice-chair filled by W. Williamson Esq. (44). Very little was drunk but some very able and noble speeches were made. The chief speakers were Revds J. Hart and Atkin, Capt. Smith, Messrs Lomas, Banks, Milburn etc. The dinner was served by Dixon Gatenby.

23 May 1849 : Busy managing the tea tables for the soiree. We erected 18 tables and then cast lots who should preside at each table. In the afternoon the music classes had a rehearsal and at five o'clock, when I should have got home to get dressed, we had a small platform to erect in the school room. I however managed to get dressed and back before tea. The tea was well served, with a profusion of everything nice. The tables were on a new plan and were set up in the saloon and the new reading room. After tea the company walked into the gardens whilst in the school room we got our violins tuned and soon drew a roomful of people. We played three or four pieces and Miss Barwick sang three songs. The class was highly complimented by the Dean who made many enquiries of me about it. [After this the company returned to the saloon, where tables had been cleared, and heard speeches which went on until eleven.]

13 September 1849 : Having been appointed teacher of Geography at the Institute I give my preliminary lesson tonight.

11 January 1850 : The annual meeting of the Institute. It takes place in the large classroom and a rather spirited affair it was. The room was well filled, the platform being occupied by the committee. On entering I was hailed and a place on the platform given me. The report, a highly satisfactory one, was read and the Treasurer's account also, by which it appears there remains a balance of £1/10/- [£1.50] in favour of the Institute. The chairman, to my surprise, put the report in my hands, so I rose and with a short remark or two moved its adoption. Mr Jaques seconded it. W. Williamson Esq. then left the chair, but a vote of thanks and a re-election brought him back again. The Vice-Presidents were then elected. A little opposition was shown to the second Vice-President but when matters were explained he was elected unanimously. The first class committee was elected without trouble and my name was still retained, contrary to my desire. The second class committee were elected by voting papers as two lists were pitted against each other. Mr Brown retains his post as Treasurer but retires from the Secretaryship, which has been accepted by Mr C.J. Walbran. Mr Johnson continues to fill the post of resident Secretary and Librarian.

5 January 1850 : General meeting of the Music Class. Re-elected treasurer but resigned the office of secretary.

27-30 January 1851 : Mr Richardson, the celebrated lecturer, gives a course, or rather is paid £8 for delivering a course, of four lectures by our Institute, two on electricity, two on pneumatics. Illustrated by a great number of very clever experiments and a multitude of clever remarks, illustrations, etc.

5. RAILWAYS

This batch of extracts concerns the building of the Leeds and Thirsk Railway in which Henry Steel Thirlway was intensely interested. By the early 1840s it was possible to travel from Leeds to London and from York to Newcastle by rail, but from Ripon it was necessary then (as now) to use some other form of transport to link up with the existing railway lines. Thus the project announced in Leeds to link Leeds with Thirsk by a railway which would run through Ripon received much support here. Despite opposition from George Hudson, the 'Railway King,' who preferred his own idea of a branch line to Ripon that would link up with the lines he already controlled, and despite serious engineering problems - particularly in the area between Leeds and Harrogate - the Leeds and Thirsk Railway was completed in 1849. Hudson's opposition had been fought off and the 3,768 yards long Bramhope Tunnel and a number of impressive stone viaducts over river valleys had eventually solved the most serious engineering problems. Most of the extracts which follow are concerned with the building of this railway and a few indicate some of the consequences of its construction.

17 April 1845 : Today a meeting called by the Mayor in compliance with a requisition was held in the Court House to petition for the Leeds and Thirsk Railway Bill and against the Ripon and Harrogate junction (45). For some weeks past great interest had been taken in the Leeds and Thirsk Railway by the Ripon people …

7 May 1846 : Two parties of surveyors arrive in Ripon and commence in a business-like manner near the North Bridge to mark out the railway.

23 June 1846 : Arose a little after two o'clock in the morning and by half past three set out on a tour in company with John Tuting. We proceed to Carlton station on foot. Before we reached the third milestone on Hutton Moor the rain began to descend in torrents and continued until we came in sight of the station, which we did at six when the rain ceased for a while. Here we took our tickets (46).

5 October 1846 : For some time Mr Duckett, the contractor for the railway from Ripon to Thirsk, has been making preparations for excavating at Hutton but has been delayed by the landowner, the Earl of Ripon. Last week, however, operations were commenced. It is said the Company have had to give £2,000 more for the land between Wath and Ripon than they intended giving.

13 October 1846 : Walked as far as Hutton to see the operations on the railway. There are about one hundred men engaged - digging, laying down rails, leading with carts, hewing stone and other occupations on the ground. They have got two buildings erected entirely of sods, one for a stable, the other for a workshop.

29 October 1846 : In the afternoon I walked through Whitcliffe and Quarry Moor. At the former they have been trying the rock on purpose to find if the stone will do for railway purposes. From the latter three large carts are constantly employed carrying stone to Hutton.

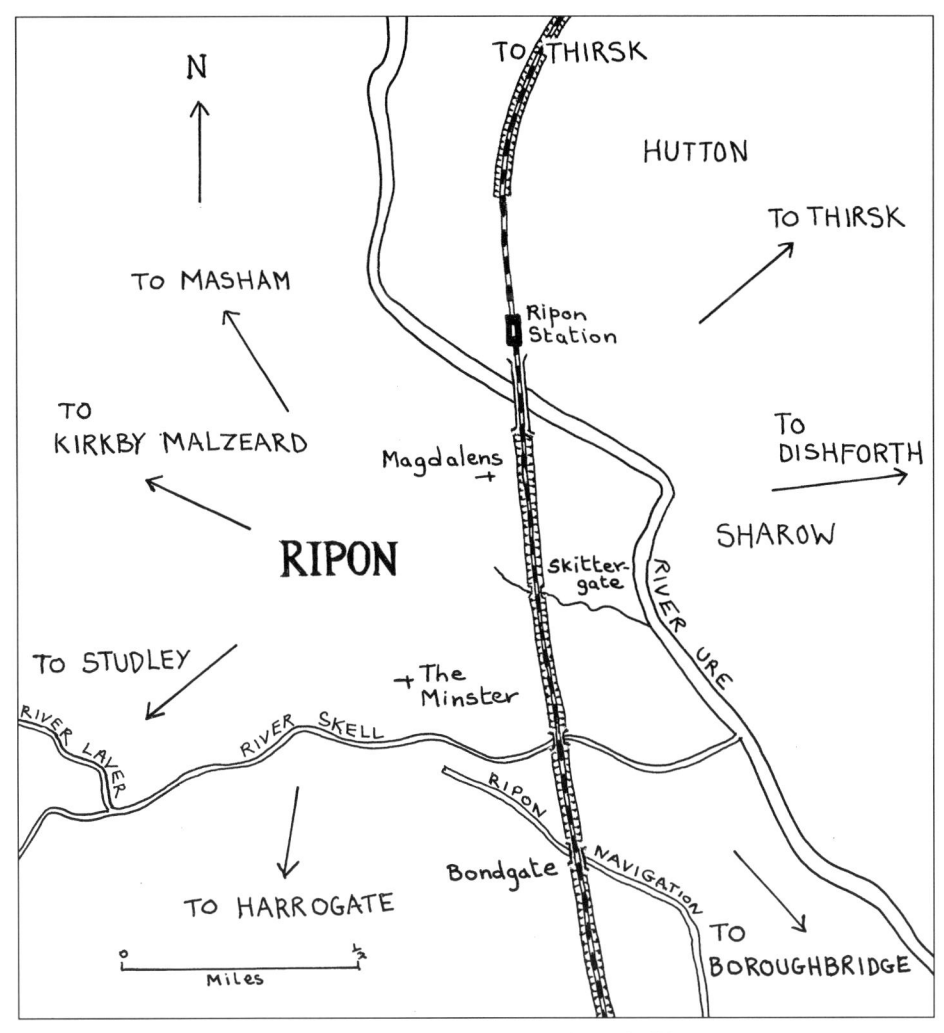

Plate 7. The Leeds and Thirsk Railway in Ripon.

2 November 1846: I took a walk to Hutton. The fields in which operations have been commenced present a busy scene. The navvies are digging out the earth to a considerable depth which is flung into wagons placed upon a temporary railway. When full each is drawn singly by an horse. When the wagon nears the place where the earth has to be deposited the horse is made to gallop. Then suddenly, by a little spring the horse is detached from the wagon by the driver who turns him on one side. The wagon rushes on and coming to the end of the earthwork it is suddenly checked and the body of the wagon tips over and shoots its load. Further on two bridges are in the course of erection over which the railway will pass.

2 December 1846: Walked on to see the railway. Much progress has been made. One bridge is finished. The other, which will span the Wath road, is nearly up. It is built so that there is a turn into and another out of it, instead of giving it a straight road which might have been done had the piers been placed obliquely. Parties have made a complaint to the Directors and it was thought it would have to be taken down but as the Directors have agreed to some alteration of the road it is allowed to stand. The skeleton of a man has been dug up about three feet from the surface under an hedge by the excavators.

18 January 1847 : Take a walk to the railway. Much progress has been made since my last visit. They are now tipping in the further side of the bridge which crosses the Wath road. They have just carried the embankment over a bog. The earth and even the highroad has been risen several feet on one side of the embankment. "The earth gave way like a sponge" and let down the new matter which was brought upon it. In the cutting I find they are not excavating to the proper depth yet, but will cut it with an incline so that when they have filled a number of wagons they set them going by themselves when they run to a considerable distance beyond the cutting. After they have got the length of the cutting they will then dig it out first on one side and then the other to the proper level. The upper strata through which they are now working is red earth abounding with large stones which when they break present a blue appearance. The lower strata is of a white appearance, like stone, but is of a soft nature, so that it presents no obstacle to the pick and shovel. Under this white strata I am told there is stone. Time will show. This morning a horse was killed by the wagon going over it.

20 February 1847 : During the week I have had two walks, one from the Navigation to Littlethorpe along the line of railway where the works have been commenced with much spirit, the other walk to the North Bridge. Here they have laid the foundations tone and their pile-driving machines are being erected.

22 March 1847 : Today the bells ring merrily - the first pile of the bridge over the Ure having been struck. It is in the centre of the river. Very active are the masons now at the north end of the bridge. At five I walked down and saw the pile struck.

24 March 1847 : I was present at the spot when the first blow was struck on the 2nd pile. This was between the Sharow road and Hutton Bank. The first pile has been driven 13 feet; the second 23 feet.

7 April 1847 : Tonight between 8 and 9 o'clock I walked down to the North Bridge to see them drive piles by the light of lamps. They are now working by day and by night at the bridge but appear to make little progress.

16 May 1847 : Wet all day. The rivers are all much swollen. The temporary scaffolding is partly washed away in the Ure where they have been driving piles.

At Monkton Moor the railway constructors have built two rows of sod houses. One part of them has been set apart for a sod church and the neighbouring clergy will hold a weekly evening service and sermon in it. The clergy who will take it in turn are Revds Poole, Waytes and Prickett. None but railway workpeople and their families are allowed to attend. Revd J.B. Waytes thus speaks of the navvies. They are a set of people easily led either for good or evil. He walks amongst them, visits them and talks to them.

He asks them to attend the parish church and they attend. He says he wishes he has a parish full of none else.

26 May 1847 : On the evening of the 24th the first cut of the canal was let off in order that the foundations of the bridge where the railway crosses the navigation

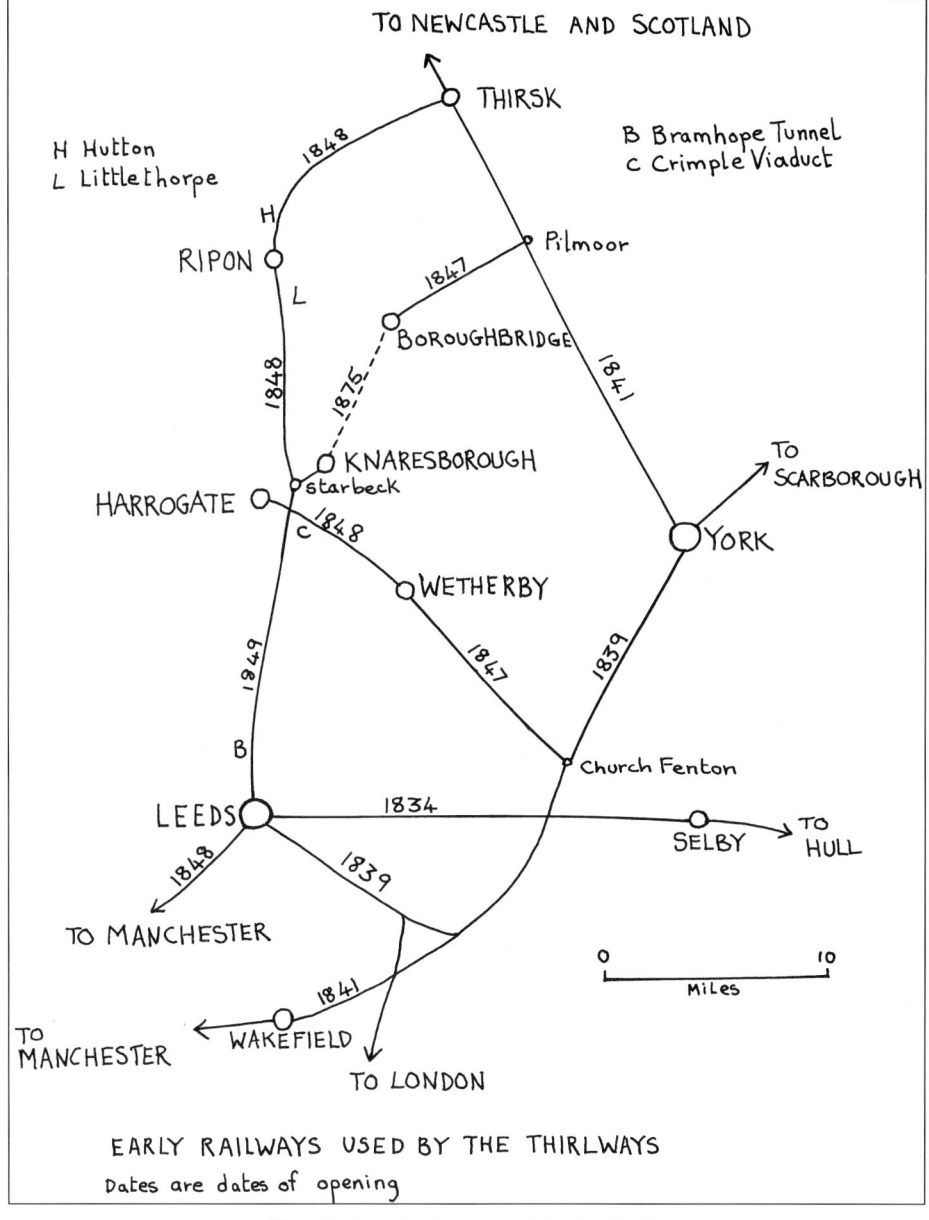

```
                TO NEWCASTLE AND SCOTLAND
                         ↑
                        ○ THIRSK
                      1848         B Bramhope Tunnel
  H Hutton                         C Crimple Viaduct
  L Littlethorpe    H
                              ● Pilmoor
   RIPON ○       1847
              L  ○
                  BOROUGHBRIDGE
         1848        1875         1841
              ○ KNARESBOROUGH            TO
           ○starbeck                   ↗ SCARBOROUGH
  HARROGATE ○  C 1848
                  ○ WETHERBY           ○ YORK
         1849     1847      1839
            B
                              ● Church Fenton          TO
   LEEDS ○   1834                    ○         → HULL
                                    SELBY
        1848    1839
       ↙         ↓                0         10
  TO MANCHESTER                   |_____|
                                     MILES
              1841
  TO     ←  ○
  MANCHESTER  WAKEFIELD ↓
              TO LONDON

     EARLY RAILWAYS USED BY THE THIRLWAYS
     Dates are dates of opening
```

Plate 8. *Local railways used by the diarist.*

may be laid. Tonight - 9 o'clock - men are busy with the foundations. The bed of the canal is not quite dry and men with drag nets are busy catching fish. The first upright beams have been placed on the piles at the North Bridge.

11 June 1847: In company with my father take a walk up Monkton road until we come to the railway bridge which crosses the road. From thence we walk along the line over Monkton Moor, then along the Harrogate road to a considerable distance beyond Cayton Hall viewing the works on the railway all the way. What most interested me was the inclined plane on Monkton Moor where by the aid of a rope five loaded wagons ran down the line at a terrible rate drawing five empty wagons up the incline at the same time, and amongst the rock we saw the men boring holes for blasting with gunpowder.

22 June 1847 : Boro'bridge Fair. My Father and George [the apprentice] go over although the weather is very showery. Numbers have gone from Ripon on foot and by every available conveyance. On Monday an omnibus commenced running twice a day from the *Unicorn Inn* to Borobridge station (47).

20 July 1847 : Walked through Harrogate to the spot where the Church Fenton and Harrogate railway crosses the London road. We then proceeded along the line of works to the viaduct across the Crimple Valley and forward to the tunnel on the other side. The Leeds and Thirsk railway passes under one of the arches of the viaduct. All the pillars of the viaduct are built and several of the arches are turned. It has nearly 30 arches - the height of one is 130 feet ... and so home where we arrived before 8 o' clock having walked about 30 miles.

21 August 1847 : Had a walk to Hutton by railway. The bridge at Hutton over the Wath road is about to be taken down. It was made parallel or square with the railway so that in passing through it there were two turns to be taken - one into and another out of it. The neighbouring gentry compelled the company to take it down and rebuild it on a skew with the rails so that the road will be quite straight.

31 August 1847 : A walk on the railway. The last pile of the viaduct over the Ure I saw them driving tonight. I then crossed Digby Cayley's grounds where they are pile-driving and building bridges. At the Skell they are driving piles. Over the Navigation they are fixing the large iron beams. Dallymires Lane they are pulling down one side of the bridge, it having given way.

11 September 1847 : My 27th birthday. In the afternoon, accompanied by Mr Thomas Tuting, walked as far as Wath on the railway. From thence we went to Skipton bridge on the locomotive which is employed on the line to pull the ballast wagons. This wa s my first ride on the Leeds and Thirsk railway. The engine (Hope No. 2) is one of the first ever built and formerly plyed [sic] on the Stockton and Darlington railway. Wonderful has been the progress of railways and the improvements in engine building since the time I first travelled the Stockton and Darlington line. The Leeds and Thirsk north of Ripon is progressing very fast. I have been upon the viaduct which crosses the line. A road will soon be finished across it. Between the bridge and Hutton a great number of men are employed. All the bridges north of Wath are finished except that over the Swale. A way will be made over it in a fortnight. At Wath we saw the junction of another railway which branches up to Carlisle. A many hands are already employed up on it.

25 September 1847 : A walk on the railway. The first iron girder over the Boro'bridge road put up today. Eight girders already across the canal.

10 October 1847 : Walked the whole length of the bridge over the Ure. The works are progressing rapidly.

Plate 9. A 20th century steam train crosses the Ure railway viaduct, the building of which is described in the journal.

21 October 1847 : This afternoon took a walk with John Tuting, who is leaving Ripon soon, to Hutton bridge. Three girders are already in their places and a way has been made over today. Workmen are busy at the temporary station. The first wagon that has ever been upon the bridge over the Ure was run upon it today. They took down the crane which obstructed the way from it whilst I was there. They will commence tipping over the bridge tomorrow. Tipping was commenced over the Navigation bridge last Saturday.

26 October 1847 : A party of fifteen started from the **Black Bull Inn** at seven o'clock - having hired a coach on purpose. We changed horses at Harrogate and took breakfast at the **Brunswick Hotel** and started again along the Leeds road to Buttersike Bar where we turned off to Pool, where we left the coach and walked forward until we came to a very high embankment which we followed until we reached the Bramhope tunnel which commences in a cutting through rock 100 feet deep. We then followed the course of the tunnel looking down most of the shafts as we went along, until we reached the opposite end of the tunnel. Workmen are engaged in sixteen different parts of the tunnel, in fourteen shafts and the two driftways. Some of the shafts have not yet reached their proper depth; in others some progress has been made in the tunnel. Out of some of the shafts a loose kind of stone is brought up; out of others a good building stone, and shale out of others. The tunnel ends in blue clay. We returned to Pool through the village of Bramhope. After resting awhile and gathering up our scattered party we started to retrace the road we had come. Although the day was fair yet an heavy mist hung about us and prevented our enjoying the scenery. We saw at a distance the Wharfe viaduct but could make little of it. At Spacey Houses we again left the coach and walked to the tunnels and viaduct on the Church Fenton and Harrogate railway. Much progress has been made in the viaduct over the Crimple since I saw it in June. At the **Brunswick Hotel** [at the corner of York Place and West Park] we gathered up our party again and took tea and then proceeded to Ripon which we gained about nine o'clock p.m. after spending a very interesting and merry day. The party consisted of Messrs Kendall, Lambe, Norman Junr., Brown, Tuting (John Junr.), Harrison, Jacques, Ireland, Hartley, Bateman, Sharpin, Blacker Senr., Robinson Senr., Wilson & myself. The party was got up under the auspices of the Institution [the Mechanics Institute].

8 November 1847 : Today a meeting called by requisition is held in the Court House, the Mayor in the chair, to consider the best site for the railway station. Two places have been named: Bondgate Green and Magdalens. The former was shown to possess superior advantages to the latter in spite of the objection of the difficulty of ascending Beddern Bank. Bondgate Green has been fixed upon by the directors some time ago, but it did not please some of the gentry, hence this meeting. The meeting was in favour of Bondgate Green being the site by an overwhelming majority (48).

11 November 1847 : Today the old locomotive Hope No. 2 passes through the Hutton cutting and comes to the viaduct. A way is now opened between Ure and Thirsk.

15 November 1847 : Sir Charles's (49) remains were brought by railway to Thirsk and from there transferred to our railway and brought to Wath, from whence they were removed for burial to Kirklington.

16 November 1847 : Today a train of 2 trucks ladened with iron rails, 2 third class, 1 second and 1 first class carriage arrives at the temporary station this afternoon drawn by a new locomotive No. 1 of the Leeds & Thirsk company at four o'clock. I went to see them start again for Thirsk but in coming from the watering place on the viaduct the engine got off the rails twice though it was going very slow. The rails were temporarily laid down and very badly laid too. The delay which this occasioned made it too late for me to see it off.

17 November 1847 : The Government inspector goes over the works and objects to the unfinished work in the Hutton cutting. In starting from the station at Ripon the trains for the present would have had to go up a rather steep incline and then down another before they reached Hutton. This was only for the present but the inspector will not let the line be opened until the inclines are made less steep. The railway was to have been opened next Monday. Now it won't be opened until next month, perhaps not then.

18 November 1847 : The Hope No. 2 passes our house on a truck on her way to Monkton cutting.

21 November 1847 : Today (Sunday) a railway labourer is buried at the Minster. He was attended to the grave by above one hundred of his brethren who subscribed to pay his funeral expenses. The navvies behaved in a very serious manner.

29 November 1847 : About 100 labourers are employed in the Hutton cutting every day and a certain number at night. They expect to clear away a space for one line of rails to be permanently laid through it in about six weeks. About 400 wagons are taken out of it every day and above 200 at night. In consequence of so many hands being employed the embankment near St Magdalen's grows longer very fast.

6 January 1848 : Today the Leeds and Thirsk Railway has been opened for merchandise from Ripon to Thirsk.

3 February 1848 : An accident occurs today at the Skell bridge. The Goliath gave way and fell, bringing four men down with it, all of whom sustained broken limbs, but all are in a fair way of recovery. Within half an hour of this another accident occurred at the station. Walker, a man employed there, was passing between two carriages when they were forced together and he was caught by the buffers. Two ribs were broken. He might have been killed had the force been greater.

7 February 1848 : The temporary coal depot being made, the company commence selling coal in small quantities.

29 February 1848 : Wet, windy weather. This evening took a walk to see the railway works. For some months men have been driving piles for a large drain which was to have conveyed Skittergate Gutter under the railway but all hopes of getting a good foundation being gone, the engineer has altered his plan and a wooden bridge is to span the nuisance. A great quantity of earth has been tipped to form the embankment between the Ure and Magdalen's Chapel but they make no progress, the land being boggy. A drain which was made to convey the water off the land under the embankment has been "blown out" and rendered of no use. The soil they tipped has sunk into the earth, raising the land on each side to a considerable height.

7 March 1848 : After an early tea took a walk with sister to Hutton. The girder bridge which spans the road to Wath having called forth some unfavourable remarks from the government inspector, the girders are at present being altered. They are placing two girders side by side where before there was only one. The additional girders used have been taken from the bridge on the Boro'bridge road where the girders are also either to be increased or strengthened. The sod house, stables and workshops at Hutton are now entirely taken away. Near to the girder bridge was built a small occupation bridge under the rails. This has been pulled down and filled up, and another bridge built over the rails in the cutting instead. A great number of men are employed at present digging out the earth in the cutting. More merchandise than was expected is brought down the line and a very considerable quantity of coal (sometimes 16 wagon loads) are sold every day.

9 March 1848 : In my ramble I crossed for the first time the Skell viaduct.

20 March 1848 : The boggy ground near the Ure has at last been satisfied and the embankment now lengthens rapidly.

18 May 1848 : The new printing press (50) arrives at the station, it having come by Goole and York by water and thence by rail.

26 May 1848 : Today the government inspector visits the Hutton cutting [at] the point he objected to before. The works are all finished in it. At Ripon, Littlethorpe and Bishop Monkton the embankment lengthens very fast, the men working very long hours.

31 May 1848 : Today the portion of line of the Leeds and Thirsk railway between Ripon and Thirsk was opened. A train of twenty carriages arrived from Thirsk before ten o'clock bringing a few of the Thirsk folks. At half past ten the same train, load ened with above 500 of the Ripon people including my Father & I started from Ripon. We were accompanied by the navvies' band and a Ripon brass band. After arriving in Thirsk we ordered dinner at the **Blacksmith's Arms** and then walked round Sowerby. It then began to rain and rained hard the whole of our sojourn in Thirsk. We started at half past four and arrived in Ripon soon after five.

19 June 1848 : Walking on the railway between Littlethorpe and Ripon we met a man carried by four on a stack bar. He had been riding in an empty ballast wagon which got off the rails and upset. He died the same night. He was a Master Mason.

22 June 1848 : Had a walk on the railway. I find that the drain which was disturbed by the rising of the earth near Magdalen's Chapel is now being repaired. Miners are boring under the embankment.

17 July 1848 : During the last fortnight about 300 men have been dismissed from the works on the railway. The viaduct across Skittergate is progressing very fast.

31 August 1848 : Lately I have had a walk every morning before work. The Skittergate viaduct is now rapidly approaching completion. This job has been a source of great cost and trouble to the Company. But for it the line might have been opened to Harrogate long ago. The original plan was to have a large drain but as no sufficient foundation could be obtained and the land near it being too spongy and boggy to bear the embankment, it was thought better to erect a viaduct on piles. Some of them, it is said, are driven a hundred feet deep and yet one row of them gave way - the row next to the Skell [sic] - so they've again altered their plan and now it is complete. I was over it the first time today.

4 September 1848 : Whilst on Bondgate Green we saw a locomotive which had come from the banks of the Wharfe to fetch "metals." It is the first that has run the distance.

14 September 1848 : The railway is opened quietly today. No free tickets have been issued.

15 September 1848 : Printing before breakfast when my Father comes in from his morning walk earlier than usual, having found for a certainty that the rail is opened to Weeton two miles beyond Pannal or Spacey Houses. So as it will be the last chance for Father & I to have a ramble together we get breakfast and start from the station at nine o'clock for Starbeck, the Harrogate station. In less than half an hour we were whirled to Starbeck, from whence we came to High Harrogate, crossed the stray and made the best of our way to the Crimple valley. We contented ourselves with a distant view of the Leeds & Thirsk viaduct, a beautiful one of stone, but the larger one on the Church Fenton and Harrogate line being the lion of the day we examined it more minutely. We went under it and along it from one end to the other. We then ascended the embankment and peeped into the tunnel at the other end of it. We were told it is half a mile long. It looked like a hundred yards. Growing bold in our trespass we essayed to cross the bridge and, not being stopped in this, we kept along the line and would have reached the Harrogate station through the tunnel but we were ordered not to enter it. So we got out of the cutting and walked on the top of the tunnel until we came to the temporary station at Harrogate.

7 October 1848 : Leave home at eleven o'clock for Barnsley: by rail to Pannal and Spacey Houses, then by coach to Leeds. Had a walk in the London and North-Western Railway station which has just been opened. I then proceed by rail to Barnsley.

10 October 1848 : About eleven o'clock I bid goodbye to the Barnsley folk and my dear sister. A few miles before we got to Normanton we were met by a man with a red flag. Our speed was immediately checked. An engine had gone off the line about a mile from this place but had done no harm. I left Leeds by coach and reached Ripon by rail.

End of October. When the railway was opened from Ripon to Harrogate the *Telegraph* coach ceased to run to Ripon. It, as the oldest coach on the road, having paced the road from Leeds to Newcastle for 70 years. When the railways were opened it only ran to Darlington, then only to Thirsk, afterwards only to Ripon, now only from Leeds to Harrogate. When my Father first knew it, it travelled about five miles an hour and occupied the greater part of two days and a night in accomplishing the journey. It reached Ripon in 1794 at nine in the evening, Darlington at three in the morning. Since then, when I knew it in its full glory, it ran from Leeds to Newcastle in one day. The up and down coaches met at Catterick Bridge when the passengers dined. The *Courier* as well as the *Telegrap*h has ceased to run. No coaches now run from Ripon except one to York every other day.

27 February 1849 : Often take a short walk immediately after tea. This evening saw the evening train pass over the embankment south of the Ure. They shut off the steam and come very slow over this part as it is gradually sinking and they are as constantly laying more ballast on it. This piece has caused them much trouble and expense.

8 March 1849 : After tea had a walk to the Littlethorpe Gate on the Leeds and Thirsk railway. A coal depot has been established here, and from here a very great quantity of tiles are sent away weekly.

5 April 1849 : Walked down to the railway station carpet bag in hand and by the train 5.30 p.m. start for old Ebor. The first nine miles in a Penny-a-Miler and then from Thirsk in the mail train.

28 May 1849 : Today about 200 persons from Stockton on Tees visit Ripon by an excursion train in order to congratulate us on our new Institute and to see Fountains Abbey.

6 July 1849 : Today the government inspector goes over the contracts [for those sections] on the Leeds and Thirsk line that have not been opened. After inspecting the Leeds contract, the Bramhope tunnel, the Wharfedale viaduct etc. he came to Ripon to examine the Ure viaduct, as on his last visit he had suggested some beams be laid between the rails. All being satisfactory the line is allowed to be opened.

9 July 1849 : The shareholders in three long trains make a trip along the entire length of the line from Leeds to Thirsk, where luncheon for 800 was provided, and to which 1,500 made themselves welcome. After a few hours in Thirsk the trains returned to Leeds.

23 July 1849 : Today we have had the first excursion visit from Leeds (under the title of the Sunday School Union trip). The party consisted of between 2 and 3,000 persons. The Dean threw open the cathedral and the scholars of the Union were admitted gratis to Fountains Abbey but the teachers and all other persons had to pay the one shilling each.

27 March 1851 : Today Mr Cooke of Leicester (51) who for the last ten years has been conducting excursion trains to all parts of England and into Scotland and Ireland, advertised a meeting to be held in the Court House at noon, but as no one went to hear him he adjourned to the Corn Market where, at two o'clock, he held forth on the top of an ale barrel. His object in coming to Ripon is to announce excursion trains along the Midland Rail to the Exhibition (52) and to appoint an agent for the receiving of instalments. Mr C. is, I fancy, employed by the Midland Company who wish to forestall as much ground as possible, they having quarrelled with the Great Northern. Mr C.'s visit will in all probability be the means of breaking up the Exhibition Club at the Institute which was not well pleased and has never been prosperous.

6. CELEBRATIONS

CHRISTMAS AND NEW YEAR

January 7 1838 : Sunday ... The churches as is usual at Christmas were decorated with evergreens. The Cathedral decorations were on the whole better than usual. The most beautiful was an arch formed over the entrance into the choir which tonight when we left church, it being dark, was lit up by candles being placed in the empty niches of the screen and in the greens which gave it a pretty effect.

December 24 1838 : Christmas Eve. We had as usual our supper at Christmas Eve of frumenty (53), cheese and cake with the usual ule [sic] log in the fire and ule candles burning etc.

December 25 1838 : Christmas Day. I was awakened early this morning by the singers parading the streets and with the boys shouting for their Christmas boxes.

December 25 1842 : Christmas Day. Sunday. Was awoke in the morning by a party of young men (for the High Chapel (54)) with violins, flute, tramboune [sic] etc. singing and playing Christmas hymns.

January 1 1843 : Was awoke before the year was an hour old by the Wesleyan Methodists singing in the street; knelt down and asked God to bless me during the year just commencing and make me a good servant and soldier of Jesus Christ.

December 25 1843 : Christmas Day. Received Sacrament. I never saw so many communicants at one time before. I trust it is a good sign ... Received a barrel of oysters from Simpkin and Co.

December 25 1844 : Long before daybreak the street resounded to the sound of flutes, violins etc. The parties of singers were very numerous and sang well.

January 1 1845 : New Years Day. According to custom I was awoke by the singing of hymns in the street before the first hour of the New Year came to a close. As usual, yet I hope without formality, opened the year with prayer.

December 25 1845 : As usual Christmas Day was ushered in with carols from many voices in the streets, and many were the "Wish Ye Merry Christmas" which was liberally paid for by the inhabitants from about half-a-penny each to sixpence to the lads who as usual were very industrious.

December 24 1850 : A few weeks ago the grocers issued a bill stating their intention of discontinuing their annual presents of Ule candles. I however secured a brace. Mr Wood (55), father's tenant, not having been asked to sign, gave candles, so he sent a couple with a cheese I bought of him. So this evening I have the usual Ule candles, Ule log, Ule cheese and frumenty.

December 25 1850 : Christmas Day. Father and Mother dine with us today. Roast beef and plum pudding. The beef was sent from York by Mary Ann, [the diarists's sister-in law].

The Cathedral is decorated with evergreen as usual but with this difference - no greens decorate the pillars in the nave, but instead a neat festoon is hung over the east of the nave. In the centre is hung the monogram IHS, the Holy Lamb, which at night is lit up with candles.

January 1 1851 : New Years Day. The New Year comes in and finds us sitting over the parlour fire enjoying a social chat with my brother-in-law, Mr Richard Parkin. Altho' holding none of the lucky or unlucky customs and superstitions in awe or reverence, I soon had, not one, but two lucky birds enter the house in the shape of the two Watchmen, who for fear they should bring ill-luck left their lanterns outside. Soon after, we had prayers and retired. The Wesleyans as usual came along the streets singing as did several smaller companies. And at daybreak people had their rest cut short by the youngsters shouting their compliments of the season.

WATERLOO DAY

June 19 1843 : In the evening being a public night at the Riding School I went to hear the music. Waterloo Day fell upon the Sunday (yesterday) but was kept today. The Hussars were in uniform and those old soldiers who reside about Ripon who were present at that memorable fight attended wearing sprigs of laurel in their hats. The band plays very well and pleased the audience. The room was decorated with flowers and banners, the word, 'Waterloo', was formed of laurel and white flowers which looked very pretty.

June 18 1844 : Waterloo Day. The Riding School was decorated with banners, flowers etc. as usual. The company was more numerous than on any former occasion. The band played the whole evening. Before the National Anthem was played at the close the few remaining Waterloo men were called for and hearty cheers given them. The men were :
Capt. Smith who served in the Enniskillen Dragoons on that day,
Serjt. Major Murphy of the 8th Hussars,
Serjts. Walker of the 4th Foot [2 of the name],
Serjt. Major Watson of the 1st Royal Scots.
Their number gets smaller every year. The four first are now connected with the Yorkshire Hussars and the last is a pensioner.

ST WILFRID WEEK (56)

August 18 1838 : Wilfrid Saturday. According to custom the effigy of St Wilfrid was brought about the streets with his usual attendants and band. I do not think it possible that he could be brought about with more dishonour than this year. The men were intoxicated at the first and towards evening they presented a most degrading appearance. Coaches and gigs are coming in in quick succession.

August 19 1838 : Wilfrid Sunday ... Great wickedness has this day gone forward. Early in the morning the race horses were practising on the course, the ballad singers were selling lists of the racers and people were drinking in the tents all day.

August 20 1838 : This morning the Teetotallers and Rechabites (57) paraded the streets with the Oddfellows Band at their head with two beautiful pink banners. We had some friends to dine. The afternoon very wet. I did not attend the races. At night there was a display of fireworks by G. Blackbourn (a bricklayer of this city). Sufficient to say they were very bad fireworks.

Plate 10. Wilfrid Festival in Kirkgate, 1844 (London Illustrated News).

August 13 1842 : St Wilfrid Saturday. The custom of parading an effigy of St Wilfrid in the streets took place as usual. The Bishop was accompanied by a drum and fife and lots of the rising generation to shout huzzah. His lordship was dressed in a cocked hat and black coat. At night the ancient foot race for a peck of peas and a quarter of lamb was revived with other foot races.

August 14 1842 : Sunday. The Mayor and Corporation as usual walked in procession to the Cathedral.

August 15 1842 : Monday. An Odd Fellows procession was the chief attraction in the morning. The Odd Fellows attended prayers at the Minster when the Revd Canon Sutton preached to them.

On this and the following day the races were held. On the evening of Monday Godfrey Blackburn displayed a grand lot of fireworks.

On Tuesday morning I was awakened by the trumpets of the Yorkshire Hussars who were ordered out to go into the manufacturing districts where an insurrection had taken place. The workmen refused to work and turned out all who would.

On Wilfrid Wednesday the City of Ripon Cricket Club played a match on their own ground near South Parade against the St Wilfrid Club. The City Club is composed of gentlemen, tradesmen etc., the St Wilfrid's of mechanics. The clubs are better known as Lords and Commons. The Lords were well beaten, losing the game with seven of the Commons' wickets to go down.

August 19 1843 : Wilfrid Saturday … The town begins to wear a busy appearance. Old Wilfrid was paraded about the streets according to custom. Foot and ass races take place in the evening as usual. The prizes were a quarter of lamb and peck of peas, gowns, smocks and hats for the bicipedes and bridles for the quadrupedes.

August 21 1843 : Mr Kirk, Mrs Carass and Miss Brassington dine with us and afterwards go to the races.

There is no lack of amusement. Thorne's Theatre is erected in the Market Place besides a circus without horses, slack and tight rope dancers etc. G. Blackburn's fireworks as usual in the evening.

August 18 1844 : More company was never seen in Ripon on Wilfrid Sunday. Several omnibuses sadly overladened arrived in the morning from the manufacturing districts. Two of the omnibuses contained Teetotallers who breakfasted and took tea at the Temperance Hall (58). Studley, I believe, was the chief cause of their visiting Ripon.

August 18 & 19 1844 : The Races. Shows and stalls occupy the Market Place. Balls were held at several of the public houses - to some, in the language of the Bellman (Gregg) "everybody welcome" but to others having "superior drill bands" the charge was sixpence…

August 16 1845 : Wilfrid Saturday. Tonight the effigy, or rather the representative, of St Wilfrid appeared in the streets. It is usual to carry him about in the morning, but he did not appear this time until after tea. The usual prize of lamb and peas was run for. Coaches and all sorts of vehicles are constantly arriving.

August 17 1845 : Sunday. According to ancient usage the Corporation attended Church in state. Several omnibuses etc. arrived this morning and returned again in the evening.

August 19 1845 : A very rainy day. The races took place amid a very heavy rain. Mr Cooke took his 8 horses [in] hand to the course. Few people are in the streets in comparison to what would have been, yet a many people I understand were upon the race ground.

July 31 1847 : The annual feast of St Wilfrid has been held in Ripon on the first Sunday after old Lammas Day, I should think, ever since the year when Bishop Wilfrid returned from exile, which event it was intended to commemorate, but it has been this year held a fortnight earlier, the proper time being so near York races few horses could be got to come to Ripon and harvest had [having] generally commenced at the time kept some visitors away, today has been held as Wilfrid Saturday (59).

One reason given for holding the feast earlier is this :
"The inhabitants of Ripon it did seem Thought Old Wilfrid might travel by steam," and so he must have done for he paraded the streets today upon a white horse, but was not dressed in cocked hat and top boots as formerly but decked out with a mitre on his head and in the sacerdotal costume of his station.

August 7 1847 : Whilst I write (Saturday evening) Skellgate and Bondgate races are going on.

August 14 1847 : Wilfrid Saturday. Old Wilfrid was carried round the town so we have had two Wilfrids this year.

August 4 1849 : Wilfrid Saturday new style. The town is very quiet - no coaches and extra conveyances freighted with feast visitors arrive and nothing indicates the approach of the Feast except that the effigy of old Wilfrid duly clothed with robes and mitre on head (60), attended by a rapel (61) drum and fife with old Stephen Buck for the collection of the annual tax parade the town.

August 6 1849 : The first Race Day. An excursion train from York (fare there and back 2/2) with a band of music supplies an abundance of extra visitors. To us it brought J. Acton and a friend.

August 7 1849 : Second Race Day. An excursion train accompanied by a band of music adds its share of pilgrims to Studley, the Cathedral and the Race Course.

August 8 1849 : Bondgate and Bondgate Green Races - in consequence of the great number of amusements both were held on one night.

August 9 1849 : Blossomgate Races and a Ball.

August 10 1849 : North Street and Allhallowgate Races followed by a Ball and a Dance.

August 11 1849 : High Skellgate Races. Besides these there have been other amusements. Mrs Butler, widow of Mr Butler whose father was manager of the Ripon Theatre (30) gave three evening recitations on the 3rd, 9th and 10th. I attended the first; her recitations were good but her receipts did not cover the expenses. On Monday Godfrey Blackburn had a grand display of fireworks in the Square. On Tuesday Cooke's Circus arrived in procession, the band carriage drawn by 16 horses and followed by a Dragon Chariot, Waterloo carriage, ponies - the smallest in the world, cream coloured horses etc. They had performances, one on Tuesday, two on Wednesday and were crammed to excess. To these may be added a collection of wax figures in the Public Rooms (40).

August 18 1849 : Wilfrid Saturday, old style. Another party of men accompanied by a violin bring Old Wilfrid round.

August 3 1850 : According to the new style of reckoning adopted by the Race Committee this is Wilfrid Saturday. Accordingly old Wilfrid, that is the man masked and dressed in the canonicals belonging to the said committee, appears in the streets accompanied by Stephen Buck and a Drum and Fife, and as competition is the order of the day another "aud Wilfrid" appears dressed in black cloak and cocked hat.

August 5 1850 : Race Monday. Excursion trains from Leeds, Bradford, York etc. fill the town to overflowing. The morning was pretty fine but after dinner the rain came on in torrents and it was hard to say whether the people from Studley or the people from the Race Ground looked the most lost and bedraggled.

August 6 1850 : A very fine day but not a tithe of the people present that were here yesterday. There has been no respectable evening amusements during the Feast in the town except "Mr Bunn on the Stage" - a lecture by that gentleman on the rise and progress of the English stage, and on the career and genius of Shakespeare, the latter of which he illustrates by beautiful scenery - Shakespeare's birthplace, theatres, house, tomb etc. The audience was very small indeed. The Institution loses about £15 by the spec.

August 10 1850 : Minor street races take place in several parts of the town and so ended the Feast.

NOVEMBER 5TH

1838 : Gunpowder Plot was as usual kept in remembrance by firing of pistols, crackers, squibs, rockets etc. and a fire at the Market Cross. In the course of the evening I walked up to the Revd Charnock's (3) playground where there was a large fire and the Hussar band. I went up and walked round the fire.

O Lord God Almighty, Thou that did in times past preserve the King and the Parliament from the designs of wicked men, preserve, O Lord, with the same care the Queen and all who are in authority.

6 November 1843 : Yesterday being the Sabbath no bonfires etc. could take place, but this evening the country is well lit up. I have seen Studley, Bishopton Close and Ripon fires. The usual band of music was at Mr Charnock's and the usual number of fire balls, squibs, crackers etc. besides guns and pistols kept up the noise and smell usual on this evening.

1849 : The usual display of loyalty and protestantism on this anniversary was sadly interfered with. Of late years the lads have added a new amusement to the ordinary ones of firing pistols down the passages and beating one another with lighted besoms, that of making fire footballs and to such an extent has this dangerous practice been carried that the Mayor deemed it proper to issue a bill prohibiting that and all like intellectual sports, yet in spite of all a fire was got up and a few reports were heard.

1852 : The bonfire, squibs and wheels, besoms and tar balls as usual. Had a small display ourselves to amuse Master Henry (62) and perhaps ourselves. Master H. quite excited.

1854 : I read a paper at T.C.Y.M.S. (63) - subject "Should we remember the fifth of November?" An animated discussion follows.

CORONATION DAY OF QUEEN VICTORIA

June 28 1838 : Coronation Day of Queen Victoria … The day at Ripon was observed as a general holiday to the poorer classes. Upwards of £100 was subscribed for the poor which was given away the day before the Coronation. To every poor man and woman one shilling, every child sixpence, that they might enjoy themselves as well as the rich.

The morning was ushered in with a merry peal from the bells. The day was observed by the shops being closed and business suspended at 2 o'clock, a procession to church in the afternoon, and at night by dinners and a ball … The procession began to move from Low Skellgate. The following is the order. The Band of Yorkshire Hussars together with the Ripon Squadron, the halbert men, constables etc. with the Corporation followed by the clergy, gentry etc., the Odd Fellows, the Foresters, the Gardeners, the Teetotallers, the Operatives' Conservative Association, the Bluecoat School, the National Schools, the

TO THE
Worshipful the Mayor
OF THE
CITY OF RIPON.

WE, the undersigned, request your Worship will call a Meeting of the Inhabitants of the City and Neighbourhood of Ripon, for the purpose of taking into consideration the best plan of celebrating the approaching

CORONATION
OF HER MOST GRACIOUS MAJESTY
Queen Victoria,

That all Classes may have the opportunity of testifying their zeal and loyalty upon that happy occasion:---

Charles Oxley	Thos. Robinson, Jun.
Wm. Williamson	Anth. Buck
John Stevenson	Sam. B. Bruce
Henry Morton	R. W. Heslop
Wm. Morton	R. Heslop
Thos. Kendall	N. Henry
Wm. Farrer	H. Thirlway
Chas. Mason	Edwin Hirst
James Lunn	James Inglis
Robt. Horn	Henry Taylor
John Harland	John Durham
Henry Burlinson	John Shields
Chris. Horn	John Leckenby
Rich. Greaves	Joseph Bateman
Thos. Wright	William Barugh
Thos. Fisher	Francis Thompson
John Willey	Thos. Harland
John Jordan	George Morton
Sam. Wise	Wm. Clark
Geo. Jackson	Henry Carter
Wm Thwaites	Thos. Procter
Geo. Snowdon	

In pursuance of the above Requisition, I appoint a Meeting to be held at the COURT HOUSE, on *Friday*, the 8th day of June next, at Twelve o'clock at noon.

WILLIAM PEARSON, Mayor.

Ripon, June 6th, 1838.

PROCTER AND VICKERS, PRINTERS, RIPON.

Cathedral Sunday Schools, the Trinity Schools, the teachers bearing (bands?) with rosette of white and medals (64). The children bore appropriate banners. The inscriptions were "For God and the Queen", "Righteousness exalteth a Nation", "And infant voices shall proclaim their early blessings in his name", "Train up a child in the way he should go", "Victoria, Fear God", "Honour the Queen" and another the inscription of which I forget. The banners as well as the ribbons that suspended the medals were pink ... Besides the four banners I have mentioned there were others - one belonging to the Odd Fellows - inscription "The Loyal Odd Fellows" etc., another the Foresters' Arms and one belonging to the Free Gardeners. Also a beautiful one of blue silk - inscription - "Victoria, England's Queen, Long may she reign over a great and happy people". In the centre was the crown on a relief cushion. The appearance of the banner was very pretty. It belongs to the Operative Conservatives. All the children of the different schools wore medals.

The procession moved up Skellgate, round the Market Place, Westgate, Blossomgate, Coltsgate Hill, North Street, Allhallowgate, St Marygate, St Agnesgate, Bedern Bank into the Cathedral. Such was the throng at the top of Skellgate that part of the procession which was moving up Skellgate was met by the first part so that they could proceed no further and a slight (the only) shower falling it was thought advisable for the schools to go direct down Kirkgate to the Minster which they did and the South Gallery and within the altar rails (the scholars even sat upon the altar) were very soon crowded to excess. Confusion then began to appear. The seats appointed were filled and not half the scholars seated. Some were admitted to the Chapter House; others stood in the nave. No sooner had we got set down than the procession entered. The church which had been kept clear now very soon was filled. Such a sight, I believe, will never be seen in the Minster again. The Choir was literally crammed yet the procession only were admitted. Other people tried but most tried in vain to get a standing place anywhere. The Evening Prayers were read by Revds Poole, Jameson and Gray. The Evening Service was finished, the National Anthem sung and again the procession was in motion up Kirkgate, round the Market Place, Fishergate, Middle Street, Market Place. Three huzzahs and the company broke up. I walked on the occasion with the Sunday School.

At night there were dinners at the several lodges. The Operatives also had a dinner in their Reading Room. Mr Paul, Operative, Leeds, attended. About 100 sat down. This Society, which was not [in existence] a month ago, now numbers about 100 members. Loyal toasts were drunk, speeches made and an happier meeting there was not in Ripon. Success to their cause. It is a good one. The gentry and tradesmen etc. sat down at Mrs Lawrence's Hall, Market Place. The party numbered about 70. After dinner the usual toasts were drunk.

The young people also came in for their share at night at a ball. Dancing commenced between eight and nine and was kept up till four next morning. The ball took place in the Public Rooms. I and my sister was there. My father was at Mrs Lawrence's Hall, Market Place, and my mother had some friends took tea with her. H. Horsefield was at the Operatives. George Horsefield took tea with Trinity Church scholars.

O that the Minster was as crowded on a Sabbath day.

BIRTHDAY OF THE HEIR TO STUDLEY (the future Marquess of Ripon)
October 31 1846 : Today the Earl of Ripon and suite left Bishopton Close where they had been residing about a month, the Charnocks having gone to Redcar on purpose to give up the house for them. Viscount Goodrich was 18 years of age on Friday last when he gave a ball at Bishopton Close, a dinner at the *Unicorn* and tea etc. at Hutton. He is an officer of the Hussars and it is supposed paid a great part of the expenses of the late ball which I attended.

OPENING OF THE NEW BOYS' NATIONAL SCHOOL
December (9) 1853 : The new Boys' National School is opened this month. The boys' school has been held ever since its establishment in St John's Chapel, Bondgate, but the school having lately been put under Government Inspection a new school is rendered necessary. The boys leave the old school in procession, headed by the Ripon Drum and Fife band and bearing banners. They pass through the Market Place, down Allhallowgate and so into Priest Lane where the new school is situated. The large and beautiful room is decorated with artificial flowers, mottoes etc. The Bishop addressed the children, they then partook of tea. Afterwards the teachers and friends had tea to which Mrs T. and I were invited but did not attend. After tea Revd Canon Dodgson (65) gave an address to the parents and a short concert concluded the festival.

END OF THE CRIMEAN WAR
September 18 1855 : A general illumination rejoicing for the fall of Sebastopol.
May 1856 : On the proclamation of peace we have a grand procession, the reading [of] the proclamation and a high bonfire **(May 7)** but no illumination. And in a later day in May the schoolchildren of both Church and Chapel assemble in the Square and proceed to the Cathedral where they are addressed by the Bishop. In the afternoon they are bussed to Studley. Hundreds of adults are there to join them and the band of the Hussars. In the evening there is a tea feast at all the schools in the city. I attend the Boys' National School. Still later in May, Mama and I walk to Galpha[y] to the Peace demonstration there. All summer these fetes are continued, at one village and then another. First there is a committee, then a subscription, then a day fixed, a tea tent erected on the village green. The day comes, banners are hoisted, music plays, the tea begins and then the dancing. My banners waved at Grewelthorpe, Galpha[y], Pateley Bridge, Bedale and (Barnsley?).
1858 : At Easter the Sebastopol trophy is publically inaugurated. The gun is drawn out of the Riding School (30) by eight grey horses preceded by the Hussar band and a large party of the Hussars. At the Town Hall the procession is joined by the Mayor and Corporation, gentry etc. It then proceeds round the Square, down Skellgate and to Red Bank where it is fired several times. We then return to the Square where after it has been placed on the pedestal prepared for it the Mayor (R. Kearsley) addresses the assembled crowd, the Hussars fire three volleys and then we disperse until the evening when the Mayor entertains a large party including the Members of Parliament, Gentry, Corporation etc. at dinner in the large room of the Town Hall. The dinner was a very splendid set out.

SHROVE TUESDAY

February 4 1845 : Shrove Tuesday … A party of woolcombers from Well paraded the streets today, preceded by a banner bearing the picture of their patron, Bishop Blaise, and other emblems. Then came a lad on horseback, next a band of musicians dressed in yellow calico coats with red scarfs. Then came an old man as Bishop Blaise on horseback. Afterwards a couple in pretty dresses of green calico as the Shepherd and Shepherdess on foot, and next the woolcombers, the whole procession being brought up by the charcoal burner, mounted and well covered with soot.

7. ENTERTAINMENT

This set of extracts is concerned with the kinds of entertainment enjoyed by the Thirlways and their friends.

February 9 1838 : Mr Gyngell from the Vauxhall Gardens gave a most beautiful display of fireworks in the Market Place this evening. Such fireworks have not been seen in Ripon since the conclusion of the French Revolution.

February 15 1838 : Saw Mr Gyngell's second display. Not so good as the first. After which I attended his performances in the Long Room, *Crown and Anchor* (66). The 'Practical Illusions' were indeed very clever especially some with cards which show the evil of gaming houses where he says such tricks are often practised. He even poured out wine and water from the same bottle which is often done at gaming houses. Thus the dupe gets intoxicated whilst the gambler takes nothing but water.

November 1838 : Attended Mr Murray's fourth chymical lecture. The lecture began at five instead of seven owing to a display of fireworks which was advertised to commence at half past six but which did not commence until half past eight. The fireworks were by Mr Irvine from Vauxhall. In the course of the performance Mr Irvine ascended from the ground to the top window of Mr Blacker's house, the *Crown and Anchor,* upon a tight-rope amidst a display of fireworks. I thought the feat a very dangerous and foolish performance.

April 19 1842 : Was present at a concert given by the Ripon Philharmonic Society. The Society has been in existence a long time but this is the first time I have heard them. The piece that pleased me best was a duet by two of the Minster singing boys (Blackburn and Calvert) "The Last Links are Broken". Messrs Bates, Nussey and Gott were the other vocalists. The band was small but very good and was for the most part of the night led by H. Greenwood Esq.

The instrumental part was more pleasing to me than the vocal on the whole.

December 21 1842 : Attended a concert of the Philharmonic Society. T.S.Dickens Esq. sang two songs and three children of S.Tutin, surgeon, played a trio on the pianoforte.

January 9 1843 : Together with my sister went to see a Panorama (67) in the Public Rooms. I was not so well pleased with it as the Panoramas of Syria, St Jean de Acre etc. and the one of New York which I had seen whilst in old Ebor. The views looked old and in some places rather indistinct, although they were first rate works. The subjects were - "The Revolution in Paris, 1830", "The Funeral of Napoleon" and "View of Jerusalem" and "Children of Israel departing from Egypt".

April 21 1843 : Mr Sunter, Darlington, gave a second lecture on "Mesmerism" in the Public Rooms. I did not attend the first and was not particularly satisfied during the second. Much I believe remains to be found out. Mr S. is a very poor speaker and should not profess to be a lecturer. He produced sleep on a man he brought with him (Braithwaite) and rigidity of the arms and legs ... Mr H. Sharpin operated upon one of Mr Kendall's apprentices (Vesty) when he produced sleep, rigidity and caused him to fight (blank) and whistle. The lecturer met with much opposition. He could not produce the effects upon others whom he tried, nor could Sharpin.

June 14 1843 : Van Amburgh, the lion tamer, performs in Ripon. His tent, which is a most splendid one and the largest I ever saw, arrived in Ripon about 7 o'clock in the morning. It was put up in about an hour and fitted up with seats for about 3 or 4 hundred. Van Amburgh himself arrived about eleven o'clock driving eight cream-coloured horses in hand, his caravans of wild beasts following drawn by grey or cream-coloured horses, his excellent brass band playing. (The band was in the carriage which he drove.)

He had two performances, one in the afternoon, the other in the evening. I am informed from a very credible source that his receipts were £120. I was present in the evening. His elephant was the first performer. He walked about the tent among the people carrying about a score of children on his back at a time. He then carried his keeper on his tusks, stepped over him when he was stretched on the ground, both broad way and from the keeper's feet to his head, and at last raised his keeper from the ground with his trunk and tusks, strode over a cord above a yard high into his apartment which concluded his performance. Then came a pony which obeyed the word of command, waltzed, kicked and capered. A monkey then rode upon the pony standing on his feet like an equestrian performer in a circus at the same time carrying three flags. The pony was then offered for any lad to ride, but it was impossible for anyone to keep his seat. It threw five lads in a very short time. Van Amburgh then made his appearance in the den containing a lion, tiger and 3 leopards and afterwards into another den containing a like number. They all appeared very obedient . This ended the performance. The company separated and in about an hour there was no vestige of the tent to be seen, everything being put up and into and on to the carriages ready to start for Thirsk. The elephant walks from one town to another and passing through the streets he caused a great deal of mirth. He started for Thirsk about 9 o'clock in the evening.

June 15 1843 : Van Amburgh departs. His performance did not satisfy everyone. Very many say he is one great humbug. So much for Van Amburgh.

July 31 1843 : An entertainment was given this evening by the Celtic pipers and dancers who danced etc. before the Queen at Taymouth Castle. They are five in number, two Camerons, a Campbell, a McKay and a McDonald. They were each dressed in the full Highland costume of their clans. Their playing on the bagpipes I did not like, but their dancing is excellent.

August 22 1843 : At night we visit the Dissolving Views (68). The subjects are the war in Afghanistan and scenery in China etc. The views are not so good as those I have seen in London. An excellent but small band of wind instruments accompanied the exhibition.

August 29 1843 : the Ripon cricketers play eleven of the Hovingham Club. Hovingham took the bat and scored 52 runs. Ripon had got 57 runs with three wickets to go down when the game ended in a dispute. Hovingham would not refer the matter to anyone but set off home.

January 17 1844 : At tea at Mr Fisher's. Dancing as usual. A much smaller party than before. Mrs Fisher presided at the pianoforte. Misses C. Fisher, T. Tutin, Aspin, Smith and Robinson also showed their skill on the piano. The vocal powers of Misses Tutin and Aspin and of Messrs A. Hunter, Smith, H.S. Thirlway, James and Henry Fisher amused the company.

January 26 1844 : Tonight we had a few friends to spend the evening. Tea at six, conversation, the scrap book etc. amused the company until supper was announced at quarter past 10. After supper the violin was introduced, a few songs sung, when we adjourned to the supper room where everything had been cleared, when dancing commenced to the strains of my violin. The company separated about a quarter to one a.m. List of the company - Misses Hartley, Mour, Bailey, Pinn, Buck, Fisher, Tuting and Mrs Fall and Messrs Fisher, Bailey, Tuting and Fall.

March 1 1844 : Tonight the Amateur Musical Society gave their concert which goes off remarkably well. The instrumentalists were Messrs Jacksons, Sparow, Gardiners, Wilson, Wright, Robinson etc., the vocalists Messrs Hunter, Dockerhay, Atkinson and Burton. The instrumental music and the glees gave satisfaction but the great favourites were a solo upon the violin by R.Gardiner, a youth 9 or 10 years old, the song "Gipsy's Tent" by Hunter and one by Dockerhay "I'm Afloat". A solo by Sparow on the violin may also be noticed.

June 29 1844 : Mr Richard Sands' Company of Equestrians enter Ripon this morning at eleven o'clock after the fashion of Van Amburgh. The procession was headed by a carriage drawn by 10 cream-coloured horses driven in hand. Then followed the horses two by two with the performers upon them, after which came a gig completely composed of iron but extremely light, after the fashion of the gigs used at trotting matches, and last Mr Sands in a private carriage built in America drawn by two white horses. The procession entered the town by Skellgate. In passing our house a boy fell under one of the wheels of the first carriage and had his thigh broken. The procession passed through a many of the principal streets and finally the man drove the whole ten horses and carriage into the *Unicorn* Yard in Kirkgate which certainly was a great feat. After the procession I went to see the tent which was erected in a field on the Harrogate road. The tent looked very much like the one that Van Amburgh had with him in York. It is not so large as the one he had at Ripon. The tent arrived in Ripon in the morning in nine carriages and was put up in an hour, a ring in the middle and seats all round. Two performances took place, the evening one I attended. The band was good but not so large as Amburgh's. The riding and vaulting was as good as any I ever saw and the horses beautifully trained.

August 21 1844 : Spent an agreeable day at How Hill in company with my sister, Misses and Mr Bailey and Tuting. We left the city at nine a.m. and arrived at the hill before eleven. Part of the company walked and others rode in Mr Bailey's "affair". After we had gained access to the tower we had a picnic dinner. After dinner we danced and sang. In the middle of the afternoon we set out for Aldfield Spa, where we tasted the waters. Afterwards we returned to How Hill, took tea, danced again and returned home arriving in the city about half past eight. The country as seen from How Hill looks very beautiful. I never saw York Minster more distinct from this spot by the naked eye.

May 15 1845 : At present there exists a sort of mania amongst the lads for kite flying. As many as ten have been counted high in the air at once, but the greatest interest has been taken in a kite which has been out with 1,900 yards of string.

August 13 1845 : Last night we have had a party of mountebanks performing in the Market Place. The highest prize last night was a teapot - tonight it is an cwt. of flour.

August 26 & 27 1845 : The mountebanks perform again. The first day 30 shillings is highest prize, last day 40 shillings but no one ever got it that I could hear of.

October 21 1845 : A squadron ball to which we were invited. The room was much crowded. 276 persons were present. Dancing was kept up until four o'clock when Capt. Reynard stopped the ball in order that the band and soldiers might have some rest before the inspection. The Viscount Goderich (69) was present and danced away right merrily. All the great people round Ripon were present as well as tradespeople and the squadron and their friends. The expenses were deployed by the officers. The supper table was well supplied; wine was very plentiful.

December 4 1845 : For the last four days the skeleton of a whale has been exhibited in a suite of caravans in the Market Place. This exhibition visited Ripon in January 1839 when it was open for a month. At that time Mr Gibson, the bandmaster of the Yorkshire Hussars, died. The present bandmaster, who was leader of the small party of musicians which travelled with the whale, applied for the situation and was successful.

The caravans which contain the skeleton present the form of an hulk of a vessel. Above the entrance and outside was placed an orchestra for the band, which on both visits contained excellent performers. The walls of the caravans were hung with pictures and oil paintings inside; outside they presented port-holes, cannon etc. The skeleton occupied the centre of the room which was not less than 80 feet long. It also contained skeletons of smaller fish and animals as well as the different instruments used in whale fishery.

December 29 1845 : A party of sword dancers from Burneston enliven the town with the drum and fiddle etc.

February 10 1846 : In the evening at Mr Tuting's, tea and supper, dancing and songs again. Separated at 5 o'clock. Party of about 20. Both evenings [Feb. 9 & 10] we have danced the revived old country dance, Sir Roger de Coverley, flirtation figure in the quadrilles and the polka.

July 13 1846: Excursion to Brimham Rocks and Hackfall with Misses Pinn, Wharton, Tuting and Thirlway and Messrs Burnett, Douglas, Horn, Tuting and self. We started at eleven, examined the rocks, had our picnic dinner of lamb, ham, jam, tarts, biscuits, bread, porter, ginger beer and malt, port and sherry wines. From thence we drove to Hackfall and having spent some time there we proceeded home arriving in Kirkgate about half past nine. Took tea at Burnett's.

August 18, 1846 : At eleven we start for Studley with the addition of the following ladies to our party [he and two male Tutings had been to Studley the previous day]: Mrs Oliver, Mrs Needell and Misses Leyland, Tuting and Thirlway. We have also the company of Mr Tuting Snr. After proceeding round the grounds and abbey we take a picnic dinner under the trees, run races, play at leap frog and dance and after all make three voyages on the water in a boat. When we are surprised by a shower the ladies are handed into the cab and we make our way home as fast as we can. Take tea at the Tutings and see Misses Leyland home in company with T. Tuting.

July 2 1847 : Picnic at Studley ... During the lifetime of Mrs Lawrence every party conducted round the grounds was expected to give half a crown, but not more, be the party large or small, but now by order of Earl de Grey every person is charged one shilling - except the tenantry and tradespeople who on application receive a ticket from Capt. Smith with which on paying the old fee parties are admitted as usual.

July 26 1847 : I was awoke early by the playing of a cornet and shortly after five the cricket players from the City of Ripon Cricket Club started from ***The Green Dragon*** in a coach and four attended by music for Leyburn.

August 3, 1847 : Wilfrid Tuesday. Had a game of cricket in the morning and went to the concert of Ethiopian Serenaders in the evening. Had the pleasure of seeing four ladies home.

October 8 1847 : After the concert ... a ball took place. Sister and I did not leave until near five o'clock in the morning but it was kept up a full hour later. [He was up again by 7 am to see an eclipse of the sun.]

February 11 1848 : The Musical Society hold their annual ball. 29 lords and 36 ladies of creation were present. Dancing was kept up with great spirit until 6 o'clock next morning. Above 30 dances were gone through, all of which I danced except one waltz.

August 7 & 8 1847 : The Race Days. Plenty of bustle. There is a new feature in the Market Place, a square booth in which are taken "a likeness" for 3d.

December 22 1847 : Attended the Hussar Ball. I was accompanied by the three Misses Buck and Miss Bentham whom I called upon. Dancing was kept up with spirit until five o'clock. The ball was attended by 42 ladies and 58 gentlemen, besides 10 officers of the regiment. The ball was everything that a ball can be but all can be said of them, after all, they are but unsatisfactory things, now to one at least if not to others.

February 9 1849 : The Amateur Musical Society's Annual Ball. Dancing commenced about nine o'clock in the evening and we continued with spirit until half past five o'clock ... There were present 39 ladies (all dancers) and 34 gentlemen, many of them not dancers. This caused we gentlemen dancers to work hard.

March 26 1849 : Tonight attended a concert in the Public Rooms. The entertainment was advertised as Richardson's Rock Steel and Bell Band. I had heard of it before as the Rock Harmonica. It was first brought out in London, about eight years ago. The instrument consists of a number of pieces of slatey rock, the produce of a mountain in Cumberland. The pieces are tuned so that each piece produces a note. They are laid upon ropes supported by a wooden frame, side by side with their ends to the performer, like the keys of a pianoforte, but with this difference all that are on the first level are natural, the flats and sharps are placed on the next level about two feet from the others and above them their ends hanging over so that they can be struck underneath. The instrument is three or four yards long and is played by three performers. Each has two mallets covered with wash leather with which they strike the notes. On a third level are pieces of steel arranged in the same manner and above these are the bells.

November 26, 1849 : Walked in at "half play" to the Public Rooms to see and hear the female Serenaders. These ladies (seven in number) are or pretend to be Americans. When they first appeared in London they had black faces, now they are content with a little rouge. They are dressed when singing in the fanciful costume of the North American Indian women. Some of their songs are nigger melodies; others belong to the copper coloured tribes, but neither dress nor songs are correct but merely got up to please the eye and to catch the ear. Their instruments are a seraphine, two banjos, two tambourines, castinets and bells. Their songs are "Mary Blame", "Old Joe" and others of that class with parodies on some opera songs etc. as "I dreamt that I dwelt" etc. which they sing with great taste. The concert concluded with "A good time coming, gals", a parody on Henry Russell's song.

December 7 1849 : Waited upon Mr Craig, the phrenologist, for the purpose of having a register of my phrenological organs drawn out. After he had manipulated my head he pointed out the weak parts of my character, and how I might best overcome them. On the whole perhaps he was correct. Although a keen observer of my own motives and powers he struck up some points quite new to me.

October 25 1850 : Sold a small violin that father purchased for me when a boy and on which I have played ever since. The purchase was made of Dick Hawkswell, Dickey Thompson's gig driver. Dick had it instead of money from the maker, Dearlove, who had a shop for the sale of musical instruments etc. in Ripon which did not answer for him. The fiddle I sold to Mr Carter, Watchmaker, for his son. Thus I have taken the advice offered in the nursery rhyme "Harry come sell the fiddle" etc. (70). But I must add I did not sell it until I got a bigger and better one but which I am equally disposed to part with if my wife wants a new gown.

November 21 1850 : More shows arrive and at night there is a promenade concert such as rarely occurs in Ripon. A collection of wax figures are accompanied by a good band of music and being stationed directly opposite Wombwell's (71) excellent band we get the benefit of their rivalry. One band plays one tune and is immediately answered by the other. Thus Wombwell's plays the "Hallelujah Chorus", Wax Works play "The Heavens are telling" and so on with song, dance and sacred airs.

March 15 1851 : We have had Gerhardt's Theatre playing to crowded houses. So well have they been patronised that they had their booth enlarged, their front painted. H. Todd has painted them a new drop scene and C.J. Walbran written them a play, "The Bride of Milan" or "The Noble and the Seer" which is being played the second time while I write.

November 7 1851 : At the invitation of Mr Ascough I accompany him for a day's shooting to Grewelthorpe. We first range Spring Hill farm and unsuccessful with Mr Imeson who all along assures us we have come up over late. After dinner we go to Fearby and range the Imesons' land there but we only put up one hare which Mr Imeson does not hit.

June 5 1854 : Whit Monday. In company with the Botanical Class (Young Men's Society) take a ramble up the banks of the river Laver botanizing. Take tea in a cottage called 'Witch of the Wood'.

8. WEATHER AND SOCIAL CONDITIONS

It may seem odd to put these two topics together but after reading the first few extracts it will become apparent why it has not been possible to separate them.

1 January 1838 : On the 27th of Decr rose the rivers etc to an unusual height which occasioned a great deal of damage and in some instances loss of life, especially at Bradford and its vicinity. At Ripon the Skell did damage to the pleasure grounds at Studley tho' not to a great extent. Several houses by the waterside were inundated and at one time it made its way into the kitchens and cellars of Col. Johnstone and T. Collings Esqr., South Parade. The walk running along the Skell from Borrage to Bondgate was in places washed away and in other places sadly damaged. Two small wooden bridges, the one connecting Bondgate Green with Low St Agnesgate and the other on Fisher Green were torn up and taken away by the flood. Several gardens and fields were much damaged either by it washing away the soil or covering them with sand, but in some places the loss was more severe - cattle, hay, turnips and wood were washed away. The Ure also did much damage and during the night Hewick Bridge was impassable.
[January 1838, however, saw very cold and snowy weather.]

27 January 1838 : The frost and snow remains. Several wild ducks have emigrated to our streams and some have entered the farmyards and fed with the domestic ducks. Wild geese also have settled very near us. Three swans came up the Ure, two of which were shot.

20 February 1838 : The frozen-up watermen (72) paraded the streets with banner etc and as usual called to melt at every public house they came at.

23 February 1838 : The storm continues much to the distress of the poorer classes who are out of work. Several tradesmen have given away soup etc during the week. A requisition signed by several clergymen and magistrates was yesterday sent to the Mayor wishing him to call a meeting of the inhabitants etc to take into consideration the best means for relieving the poor. Accordingly the Mayor called a meeting which was held today in Mrs Lawrence's Hall, Market Place (28), when a committee was formed, resolutions agreed upon etc. Subscriptions to the amount of £120 were made in the room. It is intended by the meeting that coal, food and clothing be sold at reduced prices etc or given to the deserving poor and that an establishment shall be formed for the sale of soup at 1 penny per quart. The Bishop was in the chair. Since the meeting gentlemen are soliciting subscriptions. May this meet with as good success as at the meeting. £120 I consider to be a very liberal sum and may this society benefit those poor people who, owing to the severe and long continued storm, have been so much distressed. A many of them have not obtained a full week's wages since the storm set, now seven weeks ago.

24 February 1838 : Seventy gallons of soup have been sold today at one penny per quart. The soup was made in Mr Nicholson's (the Town Clerk's) brewhouse, Water

Skellgate. The subscription is going on very well. No abatement has taken place in the weather ... it has been snowing very fast all the day, at times mixed with rain. The snow has never been so deep as it is today which still keeps the poor labourers from their work, thus a great deal of distress prevails. They have now been out of work seven weeks, during which time the snow has never been off the earth.

26 February 1838 : Soup has been sold again today to the amount of 94 gallons. More could have been sold. The people complained that it was not as good as it should have been on Saturday but today has given satisfaction. On Saturday meal and flour was given to the poor by the same society.

27 February 1838 : More snow. There is no coals to sell on Bondgate Green (73). The subscription of the society now amounts to £252 - 11s - 0d, a very handsome sum.

3 March 1838 : Thaw. Soup is now sold three times a week to the poor.

10 March 1838 : The fields are now again their original colour. The ice and snow have disappeared together and the atmosphere is a great deal warmer. The subscription list of the Society for the Relief of the Poor is still open. Upwards of £300 have been given.

24 March 1838 : In my walks I find the flood last December has done more damage than I knew of. The Skell Crooks Dam is washed down and the bed of the river from the dam to the river's junction with the Laver is quite altered. Where the river formerly ran is now a ridge of sand which has been washed down from above the dam.

26 January 1845 : Last night the wind began to blow very hard and it blew all night. About six o'clock this morning Mr. Sayer's swing sign bearing pictures of the *Coach and Horses* (74) was blown into pieces, parts of it blown entirely away ... the gas lamps suffered much.

10 June 1845 : Tonight walked to Hutton to see the effects of the whirlwind. It has split and twisted up the branches of four oak trees, stripped a cowhouse of the tiles and scattered them with great force over a field. Some fell at the distance of 200 yards. It has visited almost every orchard and done considerable damage. The whole took place in less than 10 minutes.

8 July 1845 : This afternoon Ripon was visited by no less than three thunderstorms. The first was accompanied by hailstones larger than ever I remember to have seen before. I fully expected our office windows would have been broken. At Studley the hot house windows suffered severely as they did in other places.

29 August 1846 :[The Feast of St Wilfrid was held in mid-August at that time] ... almost all the corn near Ripon was cut before Wilfrid. The wet weather of last week has caused a good deal of it to sprout. The crops are about an average. The disease amongst the potatoes has become very alarming. Fruit is very scarce. Apples are a bad crop, scarcely any pears. Plums and other wall fruit are in some instances quite a failure. The little fruit which is brought to market is not of good quality but fetches very high prices.

18 December 1846 : The snow continues ... I have seen drifts as high as myself. The mails are delayed an hour or two every day and the luggage train which quitted London on Monday morning containing a parcel for us did not reach Leeds until Thursday.

3 February 1847 : Lately the funds of the Provision Society have run very low, so today two concerts, the profits to be given to the Society, were given in the Public Rooms.

9 February 1847 : Last week at a meeting of the Provision Society it was resolved to open a soup kitchen. Today it was brought into operation. Those poor people who had a ticket got a quart of soup gratis. Those who had no ticket had to pay a penny for the same quantity. Soup will be regularly served out on Tuesdays and Fridays during the cold weather.

11 December 1847 : During the week much rain has fallen. Today the Ure is very much swollen indeed. Much illness prevails at present all over the country. There is a great deal in our town. In Stammergate no less than 40 people are ill, some of them [have black typhus. *These three words have required reconstruction.]*

H.S. Thirlway's Journal includes his comments on a paper on **Health of Towns** given by Mr Lambe on 15 April of this year.

Cleanliness is conducive to health there can be no doubt. I think that it is a matter with which Government ought to interfere. Many of the poorer classes are very dirty in their habits - lazy and careless about these matters - yet there are many I dare say who would attend better to cleanliness if they had it more in their power. At present the crowded state of their habitations and the want of a large supply of water are hindrances which they cannot remove, whilst the eagerness of men to make much of a little ground who are building for the poor is also an evil which none but the strong arm of the law can prevent.

Our Board of Highways were highly praised and certainly they deserve it. Knaresboro' will not bear comparison with Ripon in point of cleanliness. Its open channels and repositories of dirt are many, many years behind the clean-looking streets of Ripon. The town was not a dirty one before the establishment of the Board but certainly the many improvements effected by this body entitle them to commendation.

The Water Works at Ripon (75) were spoken against and certainly not without cause. The water is only to be obtained at the taps for a short time each day. It is very often so muddy as to be unfit for use - at all times the water is not so pure as it might be, for the Works are below instead of above a greater part of the town.

Ripon being built upon red sandstone and upon hilly ground is very dry. The population not very large, we have no crowded courts and alleys, and altogether [it] is a very healthy town. The cholera which carried off so many inhabitants in the neighbouring towns did not visit Ripon, although it spread through the length and breadth of the kingdom.

26 September 1849 : During the last few months cholera and diarrhoea have been making sad ravages in London, Hull, Leeds and many other large towns and villages ... . At Ripon we have great causes for thankfulness in that during the present season of sickness and great mortality and in 1832 at the first visitation of the cholera Ripon has been spared. Let us give thanks to whom it is due.

21 October 1849 : During the week the scarlet fever has been very prevalent in Ripon amongst the children. During the time the cholera was raging in other parts of Yorkshire there was never less illness in Ripon for a long period but since that time typhus and other fevers have been very bad, but the scarlet fever is very mild.

5 July 1849 : About ten o'clock indications of an approaching thunderstorm are heard but until three nothing transpires, but after that with an interval of an hour or so about five o'clock we experience one of the most fearful thunderstorms I remember. The rain fell in sheets, the darkness was very great, the lightning and thunder very terrible. The electric fluid struck an house in High Skellgate (Constantine's, the butcher's), broke in the roof, broke the windows and so descended. In the Market Place the electric fluid struck the Post Office (76) ; it entered by the garret, ran along the bell wires, broke some squares in Mr Judson's window and finally made its exit through the wall opposite Mr Ascough's, breaking him two squares. Other buildings were struck and a cow killed at Bishopton Close. Rainton appears to have suffered worst from the hail. Hardly a house without many squares broken. Mr P. Stevenson had no less than 75 broken. (We had our rollers melted.)

September 1854 : The weather during the whole of summer has been [so] exceeding fine and droughty that our streams have not been so dry for 40 years. The harvest has been abundant ... Cholera has raged in many parts of the country. London, Middlesbrough and West Hartlepool have suffered much. There have been at least six deaths among ourselves. We had never been visited by cholera before.

9. POLITICS AND LOCAL ADMINISTRATION

The years of the Thirlway journal were a relatively quiet period in politics compared with the turmoil of the early 1830s, so that only once in the parliamentary elections of this time did the Tories, whom the Thirlways supported, meet with any official opposition in Ripon.

It should be remembered that Ripon still had two members of parliament during this period, but some of the elections were bye-elections caused by the withdrawal of one of the existing members. Electors were householders rated at £10 a year or over. Local people with the correct qualifications could also vote for the West Riding members of Parliament.

Information necessary for the understanding of the extracts concerned with local administration is supplied in the notes.

March 12 1843 : Today it is publically made known that our worthy Member of Parliament, T. Pemberton Esqr., resigns his seat. He is retiring from public life and about to be married to a widow (77).

March 14 1843 : The writ for the election is read and Mr Smith, a candidate, arrives. Mr Smith is an Irishman and Attorney-General for his native country. He would have been elected for the University of Dublin, but he would not promise them to support the Educational Society in Parliament because he could not or would not go beyond Sir Robert Peel's government. The University give him a most excellent character, so does Sir R. Peel.

Mr Smith's father and grandfather were both Irish judges.

About half-past eight we commence to set Mr Smith's address.

March 15 1843 : Printed the address. Mr Smith speaks and commences his canvass.

March 18 1843 : Nomination Day. Thomas Berry Cusack Smith, Attorney-General for Ireland, is returned without opposition.

March 26 1843 : Chairing Day (78). The procession was headed by the Yorkshire Hussars' Band followed by seven banners. 1st the Arms of England, 2nd the Arms of Ripon (Motto - Peace and Goodwill to Men), 3rd Smith and the Conservative cause, 4th The Altar, Throne and Constitution, 5th Church and State, 6th Agriculture and Commerce. Live and let Live, 7th Religion and the Laws. Then follows C. Oxley's carriage (79) drawn by four greys, in which were seated the Member and Mr Oxley. When the Chairing was over a carrier pigeon was seen winging its way over the Market Place to the west with a blue ribbon round its neck.

In the afternoon the electors sat down to dine in the various inns. My father was chairman at the *Coach and Horses* (80).

The poor had a dinner of mutton, beef and plum pudding at the Workhouse.

I dined with my father at the *Coach and Horses*.

Electors

OF
RIPON.

BEWARE!

A Canvass having been this day commenced, on Mr. Staveley's behalf, in the course of which insinuations have been made, that a Compromise had taken place between the Conservative and Orange parties, and that each party should return a Member in the event of a Dissolution of Parliament.

The Electors in the **CONSERVATIVE** Interest think it proper to caution their Friends against any such insinuations, and beg to assure them, that it is the determination of **SIR CHARLES DALBIAC** and **MR. PEMBERTON** (to whom Requisitions numerously signed have been presented) to offer themselves as Candidates for the Representation of the Borough, in the Event of a Dissolution of Parliament.

The Conservative Electors have authority from **SIR CHARLES DALBIAC** to say, that he cannot receive any offer of Compromise from the opposite Party; and that he would not feel justified in acceding to any proposal, which might be considered by his Friends detrimental to the real Interests of the Borough.

MR. PEMBERTON hopes to be able to pay his personal respects to the Electors on Thursday next.

RIPON, TUESDAY EVENING,
9th. DECEMBER, 1834.

H. THIRLWAY, PRINTER. RIPON.

March 7 1844 : A requisition having been presented to the Mayor signed by a many gentlemen in the neighbourhood, he called a meeting which was held this day in the Town's Hall for the purpose of taking measures for the support of the agricultural interest and to oppose the League (81). The room was crowded with gents, farmers and tradesmen. The principal speakers were Digby Cayley (16) and J. S. Crompton Esqr. (82). Others also addressed the meeting. Dr Thomas opposed them but only got laughed at. The principal out of many valuable facts I gain is this according to M. Cullock. The money invested in land is £800,000,000, in manufactures £40,000,000. The manufacturers then constitute no more than one-fifth of the wealth of the nation. Many good sound arguments why corn should not be imported free were given.

March 11 1844 : A meeting was held this evening at which a deputation from the Corn Law League attended. Col. Thompson, Prentice and Plint were announced but only Plint attended.

May 13 1844 : May Day Fair. For several weeks past a paper war has been carried on between Rollinson of the **White Horse** [North Street] and a committee of publicans. Within the last few years the sheep fairs which for a long series of years have been held in North Street and Coltsgate Hill have been getting less and the sheep have been put into pens in a paddock belonging to Rollinson, in consequence of which other publicans have taken alarm, have got permission of the Corporation and other authorities to hold it in the Market Place. Today pens have been erected in the Square.

May 14 1844 : Sheep Fair Day. Pens were set out as usual in North Street and Coltsgate Hill but only two were filled with sheep. Mr Rollinson's field was about as full of sheep as in former years, but the greater part of the sheep were in the Market Place. All the pens that were erected were filled.

October 11 1844 : A Pig Show takes place in the Market Place, the first that has ever been held in Ripon. Mr Procter of the **Green Dragon** [Westgate] obtains the premium of the Tradesmen class and J. Renton of Bondgate the premium of the Cottagers' class. Very many excellent pigs were shown, several of which got prizes.

May 17 1845 : Today five lads have been sitting in the stocks three hours each for gambling etc. on the Sabbath Day.

November 1 1845 : Today is the election for councillors which was contested for the first time of some years (83). The Radicals held a meeting about a week back when they nominated seven of their own party, at which meeting they took occasion to abuse the Corporation most unmercifully. In a few days after which the Tory party held a meeting when they in turn nominated seven men, taking two of the seven named by the Radicals and choosing other five without respect of party. The second seven have won the day.

January 26 1846 : Commenced work at 5 o'clock in the morning to set an address of Hon. Edwin Lascelles (13) to the Electors of Ripon. T. B. C. Smith, late Attorney-General for Ireland, our late member, having been made Master of the Rolls for Ireland. The address was distributed during the day.

January 27 1846 : Mr Smith's resignation and farewell address is published.

January 29 1846 : Today the Hon. Edwin Lascelles addressed the electors from the *Unicorn* window (84).

February 2 1846 : Today the election took place upon the hustings in front of the Cross. No opposition being offered the election was soon over and about ½ past twelve Mr Lascelles was drawn round the Square in his carriage by four horses preceded by a band of music. No banners were displayed. After an hour or more several barrels of ale were given away in the Market Place, our new member returned to Harewood House and the holiday people adjourned either to the alehouses or into the fields to play cricket or spel and knor. Never was an election got over so quietly.

February 3 1846 : Today the electors dined at twelve different public houses. My father was present as chairman at the *Coach and Horses*. After dinner I was sent for. I spent an hour or two with them and made my maiden speech in answer to the healths of my mother, sister and self, and again another in reply to the toast 'The Ladies'. Mr W. Bayne (85) was my father's vice-chairman.

February 5 1846 : Today Capt. Smith (86) called to make apology on my having been omitted among the invited to dinner. Some of the committee men have also expressed themselves in the same strain. It was an oversight or I should have been invited.

July 24 1847 : The Parliament was dissolved yesterday. Today (5 o'clock) the writ for a new election was read at the Cross. This evening whilst I write the bells are ringing and Lascelles, our old member, and Sir J. Graham (87), a candidate, are expected.

July 26 1847 : During last week addresses were circulated of the Hon. Edwin Lascelles and the Hon. Sir J. Graham, but they did not arrive until today. Mr Lascelles arrived in the morning and commenced his canvass in the evening. He addressed the electors from the hustings which had been erected during the day. Whilst he was speaking Sir J. Graham drove up and gave an address also.

July 27 1847 : Both are canvassing.

July 28 1847 : Nomination Day. The election passed over very quietly - no opposition.

July 30 1847: Chairing Day. The members preceded by a band of music, but without banners, made the circuit of the Market Place three times. On these occasions it has been usual to throw silver to the crowd, but it was not done this time. In consequence the mob threw stones and attempted to overturn the carriage, but failed. In the afternoon the electors dined at various inns. My father was chairman at the *Coach and Horses* - Mr W. A. Bayne vice-chairman. To this table I was invited. The dinner was well served and the company very harmonious. Toasts, songs, speeches and recitations, cheers, Kentish fire [rapturous applause - "three times three and one more"] and musical cheers all added to keep the game alive. I returned thanks in a bad speech for the Cricket Club, responded to the toast 'The Ladies of Ripon' in a much better, got applauded and finally sat down amid cheers, having proposed as a toast 'Our Noble Selves'. Retired from the table at nine.

December 7 1848 : In consequence of Lord Morpeth being exalted to the peerage at the death of his father, the Earl of Carlisle, a seat is vacant in the House of Commons for the West Riding. One of the Earl Fitzwilliam's sons first becomes a candidate but at the opposition he met with at Leeds, in consequence of his youth, he withdrew. The Radicals then started Roebuck, but shortly withdrew him and then started Sir Culling Eardley. The Tories were still, until Fitzwilliam withdrew. They then put forward Mr Denison, who was to have addressed the electors of Ripon today but did not come in consequence of illness. Sir C. E. is also ill. Joshua Crompton Esqr. addressed the crowd who had assembled on behalf of Mr Denison.

December 14 1848 : Today Mr Denison addressed the electors from the *Unicorn* Inn window.

December 14, 15 1848 : On these days a poll takes place for the West Riding. The result at Ripon is :-   Denison 385
Eardley   67
Majority 318
The gross poll through the Riding :-   Denison 14,743
Eardley 11,795
Majority 2,948

May 5 1849 : On Court Leet at the prison [in Stammergate] . This is the first time I have been at a court [presumably because he had only just become a householder]. It was the court of the Dean and Chapter (88). After business, dinner was provided at the ***Black Bull***. Altho' a colt [a new member] it cost me but half-a crown.

April 6 1850 : A Sessions was held today for the appointing of Overseers, Constables etc. My name has graced the church doors as a person eligible for the latter office (89). My name however was struck off and I escape the staff of office for another twelve months.

April 24 1850 : Summoned on the Jury of the Court Leet of the Archbishop of York. After business we dined at the gaol. Being a colt had 5/- extra to pay. There were eight others in the same case as myself.

January 20 1851 : Tonight the Mayor (Mr Farmery) and the Council give a ball at the Town's Hall to which my father, mother, wife and self are invited. Father only attended - and much to the amusement of all present danced the first country dance with Mrs Bateman. This is the first ball that has been given since the Corporation Reform Bill became law. But in the days of the Old Corporation there was always a ball in August besides Mayor's feasts, cake night etc. (90). Since the breaking up of the old Corporation the Council have rented a house in Kirkgate, but lately with the consent of Earl de Grey they meet at their old quarters, the Town's Hall (28). In the olden days the dinners etc. were given, costing nothing to the town and little to individuals of the body, but since then every member by established custom sent in to the Corporation cellar half-a-dozen of wine per year, which supplied the table after business was done at the quarterly meetings etc. But now that they have changed their place of meeting they have

Plate 13. Ripon Market Place with the Town Hall (Mrs Lawrence's Hall), 1837.

become still more economical. They have abolished this law and the wine that was left was expended on the ball. By agreement the Mayor is to give one dinner during his Mayoralty and the Council are to give him one.

April 11 1851 : Mr G. B. Jones having resigned his office of Assistant [Poor Law] Overseer, a meeting is held today at the Court House to elect a person to fill the office. Mr F. Parker and three or four Mr Woods are nominated and a show of hands takes place, which was declared in favour of Mr Parker. Mr John Wood, High Skellgate, demanded a poll which was taken at the Poor House on the 14th and ended in favour of Mr Parker.

June 16 1852 : Mr Augustus Newton, the barrister, issues an address ... to the electors of Ripon. [The government had been defeated and a general election had been called.] He comes forward as an advocate of all the outside measures of the Radical School.

July 3 1852 : Messrs Beckett and Lascelles speak from the window of the ***Unicorn*** Inn; Mr Newton from Paley's (the shoemaker's) window, which he took by stratagem.

July 6 1852 : Nomination Day. No music or banners. Show of hands in favour of Newton, of course (91).

July 7 1852 : Polling Day. Poll declared at four o'clock. Lascelles 202, Beckett 266, Newton 75. There was much work after the declaration. No chairing took place.

December 18 1855 : List of recipients of the Mayor's Dole gone through (92) and many names struck off. [He had just been elected a Municipal Charities Trustee.]

71

January 29 1856 : The half-yearly meeting of the Charitable Trustees. The old women and men receive their half-yearly payments (93).

February 11 1856 : The object of this meeting is to fill in vacancies in Underwood's School [94] and to endeavour to increase the benefits derived by the boys in that school

March 1 1856 : I am elected Auditor to the Municipal Corporation.

July 1856 : The Trustees were summoned by the Mayor (J. R. Walbran) to confer with him respecting the allotment of the Bathhouse property (95) under the Ripon Inclosure Award. Up to this period since the appointment of Trustees in 1836 the Bathhouse in Skellbank has been held by the Trustees without right. On the winding up of the Award by Mr R. Telford the property is transferred to the Municipal Corporation. The Inclosure was conducted by J. Humphries Esqr. who died May, 1855, leaving the Award still uncompleted. Mr Telford, his clerk, brings the matter to a close, but not before he draws a considerable sum from us for average rent compensation (96), monies due from Maison de Dieu Hospital (97).

Autumn 1856 : During the autumn at the request of Dr Paley (128) became secretary of the Ripon Coal Society [a charitable body] vacant by the death of Mr Jackson, Public Rooms (98).

May 1857 : R.M.C. [Ripon Municipal Charity] Trustees - a piece of land in the middle of one of our fields belonging to the Maison de Dieu Hospital is offered for sale by auction and is purchased by the Trustees.

November, 1857 : I in company with Mr R. Lumley, T. Easter and W. Wells am elected councillor over a very strong opposition - Bateman, Gowing etc. Cabs, buses, banners, bands, extortion for dinner (99).

1858 : The Corporation ... become the agents for the collecting of tolls of the markets and fairs for the Ecclesiastical Commissioners whose property they are (100). Upon this I am elected on the Tolls Committee. Our chief object in assuming this office is to lower the tolls for fruit etc. and to remove the cattle fairs into a field in Blossomgate, both of which objects we accomplish and May Fairs for cattle and sheep are for the first time in the Treasurer's Garth.

September 1859 : The gold chain and badge purchased by public subscription is formally presented to the Mayor and Corporation after which we invite the subscribers to luncheon.

1859: Revd Powell completes purchase of poor lands at Sharow £2,580 (101).

About this time we agree to dispose of the field behind the Crescent to the Bishop for 32 years purchase for the purpose of a site for the erection of a Female Training College. We have sold to Powell the land very dear, and considering the sums paid for adjoining fields the Bishop has had this offer too cheap. We justify the action by stating that it is for an educational purpose and likely to be of benefit to the town and further that the land was left partly for an education purpose (102).

Mr Stead, the late railway contractor, having made offers for Bull Close (103) and Townend Close they are valued and Mr Stead offers about £100 per acre for Bull Close and £400 an acre for the field adjoining the Crescent and the site of the new college.

10. EXCURSIONS AND HOLIDAYS

The journal shows Henry Steel Thirlway as a keen traveller, whether it was just for one day or for a holiday extending over several days, a week or more. This section starts with some of his one day visits and ends with a selection of his longer holidays including his honeymoon.

October 3 1842 : Walked up to Laverton and dined with Mr Shaw. Afterwards went to Kirkby Malzeard. It is the feast and fair. Took tea at Mr Shaw's and visited 'Old George Wharton'. He is above 110 years old. He has been up at Kirkby Malzeard dining with the Oddfellows it being their anniversary. He occupied the chair and said grace for them. Arrived home again about 7 o'clock on foot. [For more about George Wharton see the next section entitled "People".]

June 22 1843 : Barnabas Day. Rode down to Boro'bridge with Mr Drewell of London, took tea with Mrs Carass (104). The fair was not particularly busy. I never saw more shows. Thornes and Rickartims, two theatrical companies, filled the square, except a small space occupied by a wild beast show; near the church was a company of rope-dancers to be seen for a penny, and at a little distance a menagerie contained in four or five caravans besides an elephant which walked about the show. The bills say the keeper is the rival of Van Amburgh [see "Entertainments" Section] and a person who saw him says he believes he can do more. The price of admission - three pence. Besides these [shows] were several minor ones. About ½ past seven the elephant walked through the fair preceded by their band of music. Walked home.

September 1 1844 : Started in company with my mother in one of Mr R. Thompson's gigs (105) a little after eight for Dallowgill Church where we arrived about ten, after passing through Galpha[y] and over the Laver at Gate Bridge. We attended morning prayers in the pretty little new church which was consecrated last autumn. Revd H. Prior read prayers and preached. After we had dined, which we did in Mr Lofthouse's house, of pie and tart which we carried, we crossed the romantic gill and bent our steps to Wakehill, formerly the property of Wilfrid Piper, brother to my maternal great-grandmother. The property consists of two or three houses and some acres of land. My mother had visited Wilfrid in her childhood and was present at his funeral. At his death he left his property to my grandfather and his brother, out of which they were to pay £10 per annum to their mother. £10 he left to be given to the poor of Dallowgill and several legacies.

My mother recognised the old porch, the old oven (one heated by sticks the old-fashioned way) and the parlour. One of the houses has been pulled down. On our return we looked into the school, attended evening prayers, and after taking tea we set out for Grantley and thence home, arriving in Ripon a little before eight o'clock.

October 28 1844 : The new church at Markington is consecrated today. I set out from Ripon at ½ past nine on foot for Markington where I arrived in about an hour. Markington is a peculiar village. Unlike most others the street is very narrow.

A small stream runs through the village. Markington Hall is a good well-built house with two wings. It is now the residence of a farmer. Wm. Wilberforce Esqr, the father of the two Archdeacons, derived his qualification from Markington when he was sent to Parliament (106). The Wilberforce family now possess about 1,300 acres of land at this place. Hob Green, the seat of C. Reynard Esqr., is at a little distance from Markington. The church has been built at the expense of the Wilberforce and Reynard families and the Church Building Society. A parsonage is also to be erected ...

September 7 1845 : After dinner we all set out in a phaeton to Winksley. Having put up our horse at Henry Richmond's, some old friends of my mother's, we went in company with Mary, their daughter, to the churchyard where I had the spot pointed out to me in which the remains of my grandfather lay. [This was Matthew Steel, his maternal grandfather.] After rambling among the tombstones we attended the service ... after which we took tea at Richmond's. The house is a very ancient one and covered with thatch. The door is opened by a sneck band. In the house is a very antique and richly carved chair and a bedstead in one of the rooms is also carved ...

September 7 1846 : Left Ripon by the *Courier* coach after a quarter of an hour's preparation for Harrogate. Having arrived at Harrogate call at Williams' bazaar, Mr Langdale's Library (107) and at Mr Palliser's (108), and after peeping about at the improvements at the **White Hart** (newly rebuilt) and other things I turn my back on Harrogate and arrive in Knaresboro' over the High Bridge, up High Street, through the whole length of it and into the fields until I come to a steep path which carried me down to the River Nidd. I then proceeded up the romantic valley passing on the right hand Fort Montague and St Robert's Chapel, on my left the Low Bridge, the Dropping Well and the Castle ... Having left the valley I gain the Castle yard from whence we have a good view of the church and town ... The ruins are now inhabited and contain a small museum. In the Castle yard have been lately built two National Schools, one for boys, the other for girls. Near these have been built the Court House to which I gained access as some navvies were undergoing an examination before the magistrates for a riot at the works in the Crimple Valley [railway works]. I called upon my uncle and aunt [Thomas and Mary Thirlway - see Family Tree and Family section] and got tea with them. I also called upon Mr Church, bookbinder, Mr T. Hemsley, saddler (109), and Mr Langdale with whom I had business. Knaresboro' looks a dead town and although pretty is very dirty. I walked home through Farnham, Walkingham, Warren and Burton Leonard arriving at home about 7 o'clock. After a second tea and a rest I went to hear the band in the Riding School (29).

September 20 1848 : [He and his brother-in-law, Richard Parkin, have walked to Grewelthorpe, lunched on sandwiches and lemonade which they had brought with them and have then walked through Hackfall grounds laid out by William Aislabie in the eighteenth century to Mickley where they went to the flax mill] but found none of the Fishers at home (110). Hunger would have prompted me to have sought another shop. Not so with Mr Parkin. He boldly entered, asked for something to eat. We being perfect strangers to the housekeeper a very amusing scene ensued, but Mr Parkin was victorious and she cooked us the best ham steaks I ever tasted. We then had water, ale, tobacco, pears and apples. After dinner I was shown over the mill and was much pleased both with the spinning and weaving. The machinery interested me very much. Mickley, like most other villages, is one long, wide straggling street. The parsonage, a new building, the residence of Revd T. Harrison, is a very pretty building but quite hides the little church.

December 29 1848 : Along with Richard I start in a gig for Smelthouse Mills [in Nidderdale]. The morning was very cold and misty but the sun broke out and dispelled the mist on the hills but never conquered it in the valleys. We went thro' Fellbeck and Wilsill. On arriving at Smelthouse we left our horse with Richard's old friend, Henry Harrison, the bleacher. After regaling ourselves with cheese and ale we called upon Messrs Kirby, the spinners (111), and then went to Dacre. We walked into the mills and looked about. Whilst Richard was transacting business I called upon Hannah Hebden, my mother's aunt. On returning to Smelthouse I saw them turning bobbins. Their laithes were moved by water power. The scenery at Smelthouse is very romantic and pretty. After getting tea, toast and [?] cakes we returned to Ripon over Brimham Rocks. We arrived home about six o'clock and went to Mr Pinn's (112).

October 20 1850 : [After driving by phaeton to Kirkby Malzeard and attending church there] we drove over to Grewelthorpe to Mr Ascough's (113) where we dined. In the afternoon we attended Grewelthorpe church. Mr Harrison [the incumbent] being from home the Revd Cecil Dalton preached ... This is a new church not unlike in many points Dallowgill and Markington. Mr Pickhard, the schoolmaster, has kindly lent an organ to the church and he acts as organist both here and at Kirby - drove home after eight ... bringing with me two fine dishes of trout, one for ourselves, the gift of Mr Imeson ...

VISIT TO YORK : SEPTEMBER 1842

September 6 1842 : Set out for York with Mr Douglas in his gig ... We arrived in York about 7 o'clock. During my visit I stayed at Mr Brassington's [see Business section].

September 8 1842 : Was the Sunday School treat. It was originally intended that the children from all the schools in York should meet together in St Michael-le-Belfrey Church when a sermon should be preached to them by the Revd J. Crofts, and afterwards they should adjourn to the St Peter's School playground where they would take tea in the open air.

The rain fell in torrents all day. The sermon was dispensed with. Each school was addressed by a separate clergyman in their own schoolroom after which tea and cakes were given them. The Bishopgate School to which I was attached during my stay in York [from January 1839 to December 1842] and to which I of course joined myself now were addressed in the Boys' Schoolroom - both boys and girls were present - by the Revd D. Thomas - after which they were taken into the Girls' Room and tea and cakes they had in abundance. After all were satisfied we had some two or three gallons of tea, sweetened and milked, to spare, which was very thankfully received by the poor people who live around the school.

At night the teachers of all the schools in York met in St Peter's School when about 200 teachers, clergy and friends of Sunday Schools sat down to tea. Revds Y. Richardson and G. Copeland addressed the meeting.

September 9 1842 : Enjoyed a sail on the Ouse with H. Mills.

September 11 1842 : Sunday. I attended the School and taught the second class Mr Fowler being absent. I took dinner with Mr H. Mills and tea with Mr Tetley. I attended Bishophill in the morning, the Minster in the evening and St Saviour's at night. It is my 22nd birthday.

September 12 1842 : Having spent a few happy days, having enjoyed the society of my York friends and having wished them farewell, I took my fare at the Mail Coach office and by 11 o'clock I alighted in Ripon Market Place. And in the afternoon I started work.

VISIT TO HARROGATE, LEEDS AND WAKEFIELD,

September 20 1844 : Commenced a tour. Started from the *Bull* Inn [*Black Bull* in the Old Market Place] by the *Courier*, alighted at Harrogate and had a few hours stroll. Among the things worth mentioning I saw the interior of Low Harrogate Church. The altar screen is very pretty. It is surmounted by a representation of the 'ark of the covenant' in gold with motto 'Laus Deo'. Beneath is the text 'Glory be to God on high and on earth peace and goodwill to men'. The altar is quite hid by the reading desk and pulpit which stand before it. The new Pump Room over the old sulphur well is a very pretty looking building either outside or in. From Harrogate I proceeded to Leeds by the *Telegraph* ... On arrival in Leeds I called upon my cousin James where I took tea. Afterwards I walked about the streets, saw St Anne's Romanist Church, Barricks [sic] where I heard tattoo, railway station and gas works and saw upon the walls a select Fancy Dress Ball announced - tickets 3d and 6d, called on Messrs Baines and Newsome's shop (114) and from thence to evening prayers in the beautiful parish church. Slept at the *Black Swan*, Lower Lead Row.

September 21 1844 : At seven o'clock a.m. strolled round Vicar's Croft (115), everybody buying and selling fruit, vegetables, herrings etc. In corners tents were erected and breakfast all hot [was being served]. After breakfast called at **Intelligencer** office (116) and introduced myself to Messrs Adams and Grimshaw, who directed me to the Botanic Gardens, and was soon in an omnibus, was set down and entered the Gardens which are very prettily laid out. The greenhouses contain many rare and exotic plants. In cages and dens are a bear, an eagle, an alligator and some monkeys. On my way back I crossed Woodhouse Moor, passed the new Waterworks and called to see the Cemetery. Dined at an eating house in Boar Lane of goose for one shilling; walked through the Central Market and visited the Museum. Called on Mr Green (117) who directed me to the church now in building to be called the Church of the Holy Cross. When finished it will be the most beautiful church in England. Called on Messrs Webb and Millington (118).

Mr W. showed me through his workshops. Spent the evening with Mr Adams. We called in at Commercial Buildings (119) where we saw some mechanical figures. At nine this morning I stepped into the Coloured Cloth Hall (120).

September 22 1844 : This morning I had intended to visit one of the schools but was disappointed. Mr Adams had promised to conduct me but did not call at the inn until too late. Attended parish church and after dinner in company with Messrs Adams and Grimshaw had a walk to Kirkstall Abbey. Took tea with Mr Grimshaw, accompanied them to the parish church and afterwards had a walk by moonlight. The service in the parish church was performed in a very beautiful manner - in the greatest order and good taste. The church is very solemn and beautiful and well attended.

September 23 1844 : After paying my shot at the *Swan* and taking breakfast at nine I started for Wakefield, where I dined and took tea with Mr Harrison. His eldest daughter accompanied me about Wakefield in the morning, himself in the afternoon. The things most worthy of mention in Wakefield are :- the church and almshouses, the chapel on the bridge, the river, the railway, proprietary school (121), coal-pits, the prison, Corn Exchange, Court House and the Music Saloon. After tea I proceeded to York by railway.

HOLIDAY IN REDCAR, 1845

(This is only one of several visits to Redcar described in the journal)

July 21 1845 : Although the weather looked gloomy and a good strong north wind was blowing, yet father and I set out for our summer excursion. We started from the *Unicorn* Inn at two o'clock pm by the *Telegraph* coach for Redcar where we arrived at 8 pm and took lodgings at Mrs Guy's where we were conducted by Mr Skinner, bathing machine keeper, who is always on the look-out to accommodate strangers and secure their patronage; not less anxious is Mr Stamp, his opponent.

Although the greater part of our journey was performed in the rain and so misty that we couldn't see Roseberry Topping, I observed a few things; at Skip Bridge we passed the new church a little building not unlike Markington church, but of a different style of architecture. At Thirsk it was market day; the town did not present so much bustle as Ripon's markets generally do; at Stokesley I observed the printing offices of Mr Pratt, the publisher - it is quite an ornamental building; at Ayton, the 'canny Yatton' of Margery Moorfront [a character in Reed's comedy **The Register Office**], a steam corn mill is building. The crops of corn look well and stand well although they are backward for the season.

July 22 1845 : Out upon the sands before breakfast after which we called upon C. C. Oxley Esqr (79) saw his drawing room, pictures, books etc. Notwithstanding the rain which came on at breakfast time we take a walk on the shore, first to the salmon nets on the east and then to those on the west of Redcar, and returned home through the village of Coatham to dine. After dinner we walked to Marske and into the churchyard to see a stone erected to the memory of an infant child of Mr Nicholson, our Town's Clerk. After tea the rain ceased but father being tired I walked out alone. I saw two steam boats and a few vessels and the hills of

Durham rather indistinctly. A mist has been on the sea all day and everything looks gloomy.

July 23 1845 : A stiff breeze blows off the sea. After breakfast Mr Pick, a fellow lodger, takes a walk with us, gun in hand, but shoots nothing. This morning had our first bathe which was very pleasant and refreshing. The sea a little rough. Dined of a salmon - it weighed 5 lbs and was purchased for 4/2. After dinner towards the Tees, but had to turn back on account of the rain - never ventured out afterwards.

July 24 1845 : Had a second bathe this morning. After dinner we walked up to the Tees mouth, passing as we went four salmon hecks [frames]. They have no nets upon them on account of the rough state of the sea. After these we passed the fragments of two vessels which had been lost some time ago. We could see Hartlepool and Seaton and the chimnies smoking at Middlesbro' very distinctly. We appeared to approach very near to Seaton. [They had stayed at Seaton on an earlier visit to this area.] We did not turn back until we approached very near to one of the lighthouses built on the sands. This evening the sands were very gay with company. The day commenced with cold weather, but at noon it took a turn, the sun shone, the cold wind ceased, the mist and rain were gone. Saltburn hills were visible and everything looked better.

July 25 1845 : A very fine but not a sunny day. This morning several cobbles were on the shore just returned from fishing. They had been out all night. The fishermen bring their boats on shore and sell what they have caught to a fishmonger who retails it only first from the boat, then he hawks it round the village and then takes it into the country. Some cobbles had caught many, some only a few. The fish were haddock, cod, soles etc. We bought of the man 3 haddocks for 6d, two made us a good dinner; the other is supper. Not less than 100 vessels may be counted on the sea at one time. The air is warm. We have no longer a sea breeze and the sea is as still as it possibly can be.

After dinner we walked across the fields to Kirkleatham Hospital, a pretty building founded in the year 1676 by Sir Wm Turner, Knight, Lord Mayor of London in 1669. The hospital is inhabited by ten old men and ten women who receive salaries, a dinner every day and other privileges. 10 boys and girls are also educated, fed and lodged here. We saw the splendid little chapel with its stained glass window, the museum and library with their very many interesting and curious relics. After which we rested in Brother Wilson's house (one of the old men of the hospital and father to Mrs Guy, our landlady). The house was very neat and clean. After our rest we returned past Kirkleatham Hall and through the lanes to Redcar... Just as we had finished our tea I heard the church bells tolling for the death of a visitor's child. Knowing the churchyard would be open I took the opportunity of rambling amongst the gravestones ... [Here H.S.T. sees the grave of his landlady's husband and tells of his service in the Royal Navy and in the Greenland Whaling Fishery and of his death by drowning during an attempted lifeboat rescue.]

July 26 1845 : At half past nine in the morning we got on board the ***Victory*** steam boat which was bound for a trip to Sunderland and back; on our passage we came near Seaton and so close to Hartlepool that we could see the pier, iron foundry etc.

very distinctly. We spent several hours in Sunderland, saw the streets, shops, the bridge, the shipping, coal staithes, river etc. We dined at Mrs Kent's, confectioner.

In consequence of the death of Earl Grey they expect an election will take place in Sunderland. Earl Grey's eldest son will be raised to the peerage, who is at present their MP. Two candidates are already in the field - George Hudson, the Railway King, and Col. Thompson, the Free Trader. In the streets we met lots of little lads bearing calico banners inscribed 'Thompson and Free Trade'. They are blue and white. In one place we saw about 100 boys with these banners all marching together.

Sunderland is a dirty place yet there are many things worth seeing. In my first visit to Sunderland one of the piers was finished but not the other. Now they are both finished. On the unfinished pier a lighthouse was erected. Since the pier was lengthened the lighthouse has been removed entire without being taken down. At present workmen are busy building and digging docks. We arrived home at Redcar between nine and ten o'clock. We should have been much earlier but we had to wait in Sunderland for some of our party who had gone to Newcastle.

July 27 1845 : Sunday. After breakfast we visited the Sunday School which is held in the church and numbers about 140 girls and boys.

Revd Mr Wilkinson read prayers and preached at morning service. They sing and chant very well but want bass and tenor voices. They have no organ, but are assisted by two violins, a violincello and clarinet. In the afternoon I visited the school again and examined the mode of teaching etc.

Afterwards sat awhile with the Tutings who arrived yesterday. In the evening at church again. Mr Wilkinson read prayers and Revd C. Rose of St Cuthbert's, York, preached from the 33rd chapter of Isaiah, 24th verse: "And the inhabitants shall not say I am sick; the people that dwell therein shall be forgiven their iniquity".

The sea today has been calm and still without a breaker; the day is warm and fine.

July 28 1845 : A steam boat set out for Sunderland this morning and returned at ten o'clock at night and landed their passengers at Coatham - could not get to Redcar.

We bathed today in company with Thos. Tuting. Today the herring fishery has commenced here. Two boats with three men in each have gone out. The boats are much larger than the cobbles and are used for nothing else. About eight weeks in the year, the time the herring fishing lasts, they are in use, and then they are laid up until next year. Today we bought a salmon for 3/4 which weighed 5 lbs.

July 29 1845 : A good rough sea. The two herring boats return and sell their fish at 5/6 per 100. After breakfast we had a sail upon the sea for an hour or two and got well tossed and rather wet, after which we bathed. In the afternoon the herring boats start again and with them a third belonging to Atkinson, Mrs Guy's son-in-law. He would have gone last night but could not get the nets ready which are all new ones. Last season they lost all their nets - value £18. The nets sunk through the weight of fish and were never recovered.

July 30 1845 : A fine morning and a beautiful smooth sea. The herring boats return. When Atkinson arrives we put out in a cobble with fish baskets to carry to his boat. Whilst they were sorting and counting the fish we had a pull about on the sea for some time. We then went on shore to fetch Tuting and returned to the boat. I pulled the oars until my hands were sore.

Potts' boat brought in 75 herrings, Dobson's boat ... 375 herrings, Atkinson's boat ...1,250 herrings.

After dinner we walked down to Saltburn and had a walk upon the cliffs from which is gained the most beautiful sea view I have ever seen.

Yesterday night at six o'clock one of the inhabitants was buried. He had been a keeper of baths and machines etc. He and his sister, Diana, were well known to the visitors some years back. Skinner succeeded him when he gave up the business. An hour before the funeral took place the Bellman went round the village ringing his bell but saying nothing. It is the custom of the place and answers as a general invitation to the inhabitants. Any may attend that will. The old man has left property behind him.

July 31 1845 : Four herring boats have arrived this morning, three with 400 fish each, the other with 800. This morning I observed a singular looking vessel with red sails. I was told it was a French lugger going into Hartlepool for fish. Ten years ago when at Hartlepool I remember seeing one of these vessels and seeing the crew on shore busy salting them and laying them in casks.

Had our last bathe. In the afternoon made preparations for returning home.

August 1 1845 : Went to Coatham before breakfast and returned by the sands. We went and bought a salmon. This is our last morning walk. We have been every morning before breakfast.

The steamer that took us to Sunderland set out this morning to Scarbro'. Had it gone a day or two sooner we might have gone with it.

At 9 o'clock we started by the *Ocean* coach and after a very pleasant ride we arrived at Stockton. When we entered all the shops were closed out of respect to the late D. Raisbeck Esqr. who had been chief magistrate and Col. of the Volunteers during the late war. He was buried today. Before we left the shops were opened. After seeing Mr J. Appleton [an acquaintance of his father's from his apprenticeship days] and looking about us we proceeded to New Stockton which has all been built since my last visit. We took the rail for Middlesbro' where we saw the docks, new streets, church etc. Then took rails again for Darlington where we spent two hours visiting our property and friends (122) and had a peep at the new church inside and out. Afterwards we came by rail to Thirsk, coach to Ripon and were safely set down at 8 o'clock. Praised be God for having brought us home in safety.

[There follows a long account of the 'curiosities' on display at Kirkleatham, including a piece of stone said to have been part of the Temple at Jerusalem and a carving representing St George and the Dragon cut by a prisoner out of one piece of wood.]

We have met many Ripon people during our stay among whom have been :- Revd J. Jameson and lady; Revd Joseph Charnock and lady; Mrs Rhodes and family; Revd P. Stubbs and family of Well; Mrs Poole; Mr and Mrs Jackson, grocer; Lady Ricketts; Revd John Charnock and lady; Mrs Ostcliffe; Mrs Dunnington; Mr T. Tuting and sisters; Miss Rapers, Masham.

VISIT TO LONDON, 1842

May 20 1842 : Today we (father and I) started from Ripon by the *Union* coach to Leeds on our way to London (123). This is the second time I have visited the great city [the first time was in 1837 when he was seventeen]. We dined at Leeds with my cousin James, saw his wife and child, my sister's god-daughter, for the first time. At one o'clock started by the railway for London via Derby and Rugby arriving at our journey's end about a ¼ after 11. We lodged at Mr Jas. Horsman's, No. 9, Brownlow Street, an old friend of my father's. [It may be significant that a Mr. T. Horsman once owned property at what was to become Thirlway's Corner.] It would be useless to attempt to describe all I saw but a short catalogue must find a place here.

May 21 1842 : Having a many parcels we endeavoured to get rid of as many as we could today. In the morning visited my aunt [his father's sister, Mary: see Family section] whom we found quite well. In the afternoon Bowling Walker and Co. where we took tea, after which we called upon Mr Myalls and Simpkin Marshall and Co. [business acquaintances].

May 22 1842 : Sunday. Went to St Paul's and St Stephen's Walbrook and Christ Church Hospital. Afternoon and evening at my aunt's. Had a walk in the parks.

May 23 1842 : Went to Smithfield. It was said there was about 3,000 cattle and about 30,000 sheep besides calfs and pigs. We saw crowds hurrying to Newgate to see Good, the murderer, executed. People were busy giving tracts. I received one. May God in His mercy make a many of them instrumental to His glory. After breakfasting called upon Fred Jones, Thos. Fisher and Henry Todd. J. Fisher showed us over the extensive warehouses he is in. They belong to Morrison and Co. and are in Fore Street. H. Todd showed us the British Wine Manufactory etc. belonging to Mr Pell and Company. Henry afterwards accompanied us to the Tower, the Tunnel [Brunel's tunnel - the first under the Thames?] and to Greenwich after which we took tea with him and returned home to our lodgings.

May 24 1842 : Tuesday. A very rainy day. Among the booksellers all day. At night at Madame Tussauds' Waxworks. A very splendid sight indeed.

May 25 1842 : Wednesday. Business in Soho Square. Saw the Bazaar, Oxford Street. Saw Thos. Browne, our apprentice's brother, the Pantheon containing a picture gallery, bazaar, aviary and conservatory. Called upon the members for our city. In the afternoon at the British Museum. At night at the Polytechnic Institution. This is one of the rational amusements in London.

May 26 1842 : Thursday. At my aunt's, Westminster Abbey and National Gallery. Afternoon at the Zoological Gardens and took tea at Mrs Robson's, No.7, Clarence Terrace, Regents Park.

May 27 1842 : Friday. Business at Williams Coopers & Co. where we saw a wonderful machine for cutting paper at the edges. I may mention calling at Chipps, a bookbinder of father's acquaintance, where we saw the blocking and [?] and hydraulic presses as well as the singular machine for cutting and squaring mill board. At the Annual Exhibition of the British Academy. At night in the House of Commons and the Haymarket Theatre.

AGAINST
DRUNKENNESS AND LEWDNESS.

Extracted from Dr. Watts's *Miscellaneous Thoughts*, Nos. 35 and 36
with a few reflections subjoined.

AGAINST DRUNKENNESS.

IS it not strange that every creature
   Should know the measure of its thirst?
(They drink but to support their nature,
   And give due moisture to their dust;)

While man, vile man! whose nobler kind
   Should scorn to act beneath the beast,
Drowns all the glories of his mind,
   And kills his soul to please his taste!

Oh what a hateful shameful sight,
   Are drunkards reeling through the street!
Now are they fond, and now they fight,
   And pour their shame on all they meet.

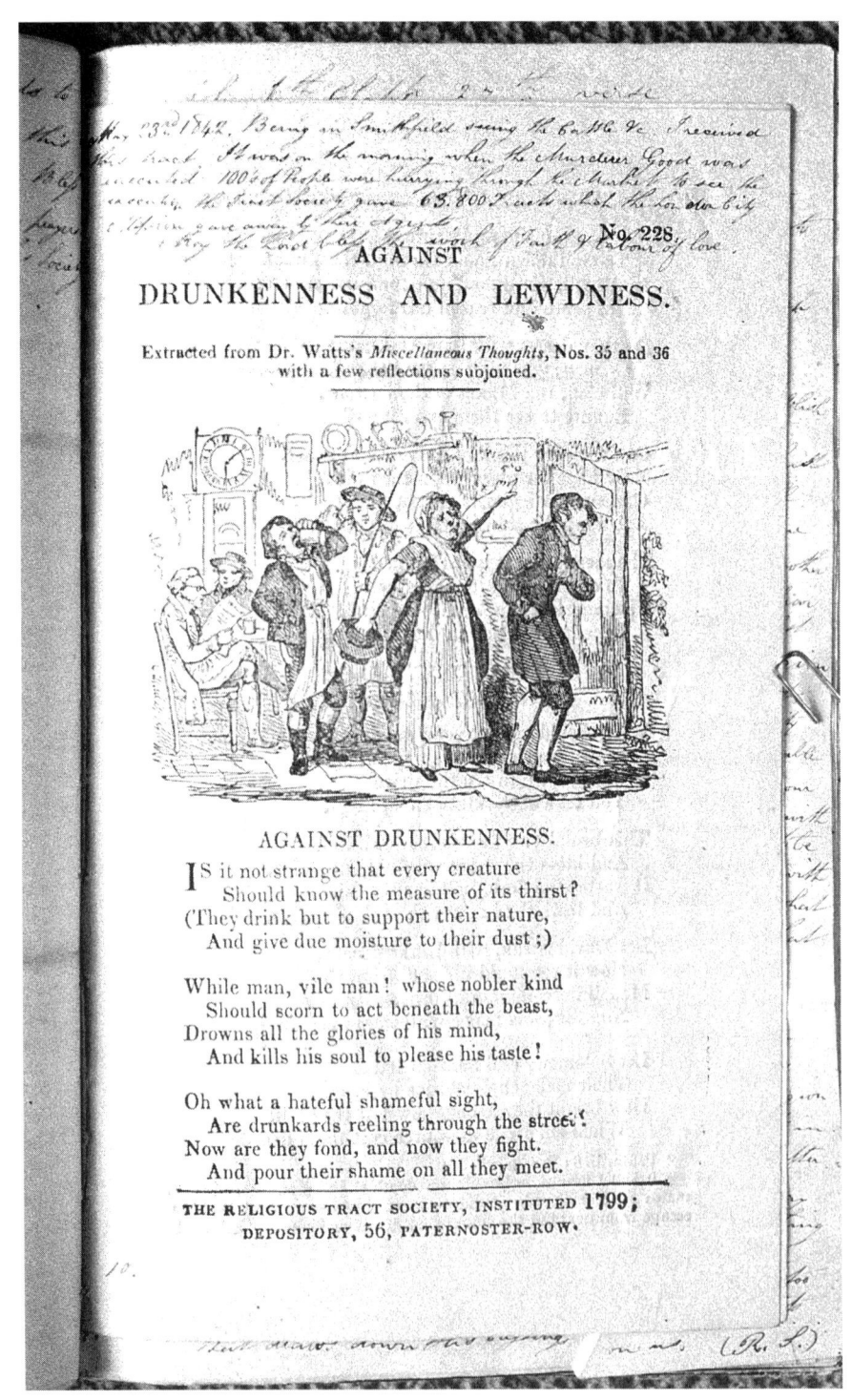

THE RELIGIOUS TRACT SOCIETY, INSTITUTED 1799;
DEPOSITORY, 56, PATERNOSTER-ROW.

Plate 14. Temperance Society leaflet distributed in London at the time of the execution of Good, the murderer, as mentioned in the diarist's account of his visit to the capital. Leaflet fixed in the journal.

May 28 1842 : Saturday. Saw the parade of a regiment of Foot Guards in St James Park. Bought a watch of Mr Bowen, No. 2, Tichborne Street, Haymarket. It is a lever and No. 4066. In the afternoon at Sloane's Museum, a most beautiful though small collection of paintings, antiquities etc. Myall's at night and a ramble to look at the splendid shops.

May 29 1842 : Sunday. At Hampton Court Palace and Bushy Park and Richmond Hill together with my aunt, father, Mr and Mrs Horsman and two more. Grant I beseech Almighty God that I may see my wrongdoing in thus dishonouring what thou hast set apart for an holy use and may be truly sorry and never do the like again and may all those who were my companions see, confess and forsake the sin and find mercy and pardon through the merits of Jesus Christ, Amen.

May 30 1842 : Saw the parade on the park, bade farewell to my aunt, bought presents etc., visited the College of Surgeons and made preparations for returning home. Tonight the Queen was shot at. As soon as I heard the news I ran to the place to enquire the truth.

May 31 1842 : At six am started from Euston Square for Leeds via Hampton and Derby. Saw cousin Henry again at Wolverton and his wife and child (124). Arrived at home about nine pm.

VISIT TO LONDON 1851. THE GREAT EXHIBITION.

August 8 1851 : Start for London. Third class to Leeds, thence by Great Northern. Finding two Ripon grocers, Mallinson and Auton, going by 5/- carriage I go with them. As we went along we had fine views of Lincoln and Peterborough cathedrals and Boston church steeple and a very different style of country compared with the Midland route. We arrived in London about six. After having a refresh at No. 9, Brownlow, Holborn, I walked down to see my aunt.

August 9 1851 : Called at Simpkin's. Saw H. Browne, the Royal Exchange, the Bank, London Bridge, a twopenny steam boat ride, the Chinese junk, the Temple gardens, hall and church, Covent Garden Market, the Great Globe, the Exhibition building. Ride to Kew by bus. Kew Gardens. Ride down the river - Myall's.

August 10 1851 : Temple Church, St Dunstan's, Westminster Abbey, the parks, New Street, Westminster again.

August 11 12 13 14 1851 : At the Exhibition of the Industry of all Nations. For particulars see printed accounts. My eyes warn me not to write too much …

August 12 1851 : This evening on leaving the Exhibition stepped over the road to Gore House now opened as Soyer's Symposium. Wandered up and down the grounds, had a cup of coffee at the American Bar, looked into the Encampment of all Nations but did not lunch, looked into the Baronial Hall but did not dine, walked the Bells with my eyes shut but did not throw at the baskets (125). From thence went to Bartlett's "Pilgrimage of the Holy Land", a panorama accompanied with music and singing.

August 13 1851 : Tonight I visited the Polytechnic Exhibition, heard a lecture on "Gas Burners", another on the "Harp", with vocal and instrumental accompaniments, and another illustrated with dissolving views (68) on the late solar eclipse - the diving bell, models and dissolving views as usual.

August 14 1851 : Tired and weary, yet very loath to go, left the Exhibition at three o'clock, crossed Green Park and so to the Vernon Gallery and thence to the National Gallery.

August 15 1851: Two letters arrive, one from my father granting me a week longer and telling me my sister would be with me on Saturday night, the other is from sister asking me to meet her at Euston Square Station on Friday night.

Had a walk over Waterloo Bridge, back by Hungerford, but missed Henry Browne [former apprentice] who was to have gone to Windsor today. Thence by water to Woolwich, saw the Arsenal, the Rotunda and firing of the flagstaff with cannon and howitzer. Back by rail ... Sister arrives.

[For the next six days H.S.T. takes his sister round London eventually returning to Ripon on August 22nd.]

A SCOTTISH HONEYMOON 1850

As described in the Family section the writer was married in York on September 10th 1850.

When the wedding celebrations were over he and his bride left York for a honeymoon in Scotland.

It seemed better to put the long account of that honeymoon here rather than include it in the Family section.

September 10 1850 : ... Before we leave Yorkshire the sun breaks forth and shines on my bride ... At Newcastle we have two hours stay which we devote to seeing a few of the streets and other objects in Newcastle. We had come across the High Level Bridge by rail. We now walk across it, examine the Central Station just opened by the Queen, take peeps into the Exchange Room and Market and then take the rails again. As we shoot along by express train we now and then get glimpses of the sea and at Berwick we cross the Tweed by the Royal Border Bridge just named and opened by the Queen. Near 11pm we reach Edinburgh and take a cab to Sinclair's Temperance Lodgings opposite the Post Office, but the house being full we are directed to Sinclair's other establishment - No. 12, South Street, Princes Street - to which our luggage is conveyed. A refreshing cup of tea and we soon retire to rest.

September 11 1850 : My 30th birthday. After breakfast we write our friends word of our safe arrival in Edinburgh. Then comes my first walk in the Scottish metropolis. On popping out I find Scott's Monument at our street end. After posting my letters I return for my bride. We walk the whole length of Princes Street and admire the magnificent street with its double row of shops on one side, and its neat park-like enclosure on the other, over the trees and shrubs of which are seen the castle ramparts with Old Mons Meg above all. As we pass on this side we see the Free Church College, the Institution, Scott's Monument, the railway station, the Old Town, Salisbury Crag and Arthur's Seat and right in front Calton Hill, to which place we direct our steps, and are not a little amused to find that part of it is a drying ground for clothes, the women (who apparently make it their employment) bring the wet linen on their backs in a large bundle, spread them on the grass and then sit down to watch them dry whilst they knit. The day was rather misty yet we had a good view of Holyrood, the Castle and the town but a very dim one of the sea. The lighthouse on Inchkeith appeared indistinctly amongst the clouds. After having satisfied ourselves with looking about on the hill at the Observatory, Nelson's Monument etc. we descend and crossing North Bridge enter the Old Town. We look into St Giles Cathedral, now divided into three churches, and then into the Victoria Hall, from thence we proceed to the Castle, walk upon the ramparts and are amused by the Highland soldiers, Mons Meg and the views from the batteries. We find that the Crown of Scotland and other regalia are exhibited here, but having no tickets we cannot see them. Before we return to our lodgings we gain admittance to the Sculpture Gallery at the Royal Institution and before the day is out we get a good ramble in the streets of both the old and new town. The old town I find often dirty and crowded, the houses of it being built 8 or 9 stories high and in some cases even higher. In the new town I am surprised at the cleanly appearance of the buildings, the width and beauty of the streets and squares. After dusk the old town presents a singular appearance from Princes Street, the lights in the numerous windows, one above the other, beginning with the lowest houses in the valley and ascending up the hill, the eye meets nothing but little square spots of light, the highest of which appear in the sky and mingle with the stars.

September 12 1850 : We have no sooner done breakfast than we walk down to the railway station and there take first class tickets to Leith. A travel under the new town in the dark without a locomotive and another short travel in daylight with a locomotive brings us to the port of Edinburgh where I am a little surprised to find spacious docks and much shipping. Nor does the length of the wooden pier deduct from my surprise. We walk out as far as we can get on the pier for it is yet unfinished and are sorry to find it is low water and very misty. Near the pier is an old round Martello tower. We choose one of the largest steamers and go aboard. It is one that plies between Hamburg and Leith. The best cabins are elegantly fitted up, but the fore-cabin is unfurnished. It is, we are told, mostly used by German emigrants to America. They make the passage in steamer from Hambro' [Hamburg] to Leith, from thence by rail to Glasgow where they take shipping to the New World. Near the vessel we saw a very great number of firkins of Dutch butter into each of which they were pouring a small quantity of tar. In the docks we saw them unloading, and weighing as they did so, corn and salt fish. Leaving Leith we walked on to Newhaven. We had been amused by the fishwives in Edinburgh so we went to see them at home. We watched several young women baiting hooks with mussels for the fishermen and from the specimens of women we saw in the streets and the weight of fish we had seen them carry in Edinburgh we agreed they were the most powerful race of females we had seen. Their picturesque dress and cleanliness also single them out as not being of the common race of womankind. Leaving Newhaven we spy a singular spider-web sort of erection - the Chain Pier, a very slight structure and intended only for foot-passengers. It would admit of a wheelbarrow but that would be about all. From this pier we embarked on a small steamer which took us to Kirkcaldy, a ten mile voyage. We landed and walked the pier but had soon to re-embark which was very tantalizing, seeing there were some nice sands to walk upon. We had Ravencraig Castle pointed out to us and more ruins, as well as a large oil-cloth manufactory situated on a precipice. In going and coming we had to pass the island of Inchkeith with its tall cliffs and lighthouse. Unfortunately the day was misty. On returning we could see Arthur's Seat penetrating the mist but the castle and the town were enveloped in fog. Having again landed at the Chain Pier we take the rails again with third class tickets. We reached Edinburgh about five. Having subsisted the whole day on a pennyworth of apples, all of which I ate myself, we were both quite ready for dinner which was soon served. The fish was most excellent but neither could tell what sort it was until we enquired, and here a word on Scottish cookery etc. Eggs none of the best, beef steaks ditto, haddocks fried delicious, smoked ham ditto, roast beef etc. much as usual. At breakfast or tea we rarely had toast and never bread and butter. The butter was brought on in little ornamental patties, not unlike a leaf curled up, and the bread in little rolls or bunns [sic]. In the evening we had a walk but either from the construction of the shops or the diversity in taste the streets did not appear so brilliant as those of our English town.

September 13 1850 : The first place visited this morning was the Royal Institution again to see the picture gallery which is only open two days weekly. Here we saw several pictures by the ancient masters as well as six by Etty, but the picture which gave us most pleasure was 'Christ teaching humility' by R. S. Lander. From here we cross into the old town again and wander into the Grey Friars Churchyard from which we gain some good views of the Castle and Heriot's Hospital. The building standing in its midst, as its name implies, was once in the possession of the Roman Catholics, but since the Reformation it has been (like St Giles') divided into two places of worship. In January 1845 this building was destroyed by fire, and one half is yet in ruins. In this burial ground lay interred many eminent Scottish characters. Leaving here we pass the Charity Workhouse and come to Heriot's Hospital, a peculiar but splendid building, and opposite Watson's Hospital. We then stray down the Meadow Walk apparently a promenade for the neighbourhood neatly planted with trees and much broader than a highway. We then return into High Street and at the City Chambers obtain an order to see the Regalia in the Castle. We might also get an order here to see Heriot's Hospital but we have not time, so we proceed a second time to the Castle and this time gain admittance to the Crown Room which is similarly lighted as the Crown Room in the Tower in London. The Regalia consists of the Scottish crown, a sceptre, sword of state, a collar and badge of St George and the badge of St Andrew alone, the collar being lost, and a ring of Charles the 1st's. In the same room is the strong oak chest in which they had been hid from the Union to the days of Sir W. Scott. We then saw the prison room of Queen Mary in which she gave birth to James VI of Scotland and 1st of England, and we looked out of the window and down the precipice whence the poor little fellow was lowered a height of 300 feet.

After this we returned to dinner, and then took a survey of the markets. We began with a Greengrocers' and then a flight of steps brought us into the Fish Market which it seems is kept by women, all with one exception being Margarets.

Their names are painted over their stalls. Another flight of steps brings us into the fleshers' [meat] market and so we go up until we reach the High Street, where we see Knox Corner. We then proceed along Canongate to Holyrood passing the Tolbooth as we go. At Holyrood we see the picture gallery, Queen Mary's apartments etc. and the ruined chapel which consists of nothing more than the nave of the original building which has since then been built up, had an altar placed at its east end and been converted into a chapel. It is now a ruin. From here we strolled into the park. Arthur's Seat was quite invisible and the mist had settled down on Salisbury Crag which prevented our ascending it. So we returned by a saunter through the old town to No.12.

September 14 1850 : On setting out this morning we had a walk in St Andrew's Square, which we could see from our lodgings. It is a square equal to those of London. In the centre rises the Melville Monument, a tall column 136 feet high surmounted by a statue 14 feet high. In this square lived Hume, the historian, and here are several banks most of them elegant buildings. We then walk along Princes Street until the base of Calton Hill where we turn into a small churchyard. Hume is buried here. We then proceed to the park, pass Holyrood and enquire the best way to Arthur's Seat. A soldier tells us to take the Victoria Drive to the right of Salisbury Crag and then take the nearest point, but afterwards ask a parkkeeper who directs us past St Anthony's Chapel to St Anthony's Well, where we drink and then follow the path. It is rather uphill work and by the time we get to the top we are quite ready for another drink and luckily a man is there before us who sells very refreshing lemonade but who has no change, so we get as much lemonade and information as comes to sixpence. To enumerate all the places we saw from here would be more than my memory could. We saw Edinburgh however as though we were suspended over it, the Firth of Forth, Inchkeith, Leith piers, the opposite shores, North Berwick cone, the Bass Rock, Prestonpans, Portobello, the Pentland Hills etc. The day was by far the clearest we had in Edinburgh and yet was by no means so clear as we could have wished. Had it been quite clear we should have seen out on the ocean on one side and Ben Lomond on the other. We descended the hill or rather mountain by the opposite side to that by which we ascended it and wondered it was so short. On reaching the Victoria Drive we walked along it by the Dunsapie Loch at the foot of Salisbury Crag and so into Edinburgh. After dinner we start again. The Zoological Gardens is our next point where an horticultural fete is being held, but we reach it rather late. The specimens of flowers and fruit appear very good but not numerous. A Dragoon Band conducted by Herr Somebody was giving a promenade concert and those of the fashion and beauty of Edinburgh who were left were seated round the band dressed in best bibs and tuckers listening to the music and watching the antics of Herr Somebody. The gardens are nicely laid out, command pleasing prospects of Calton Hill, Arthur's Seat etc. and are well stocked with birds and animals. One curiosity may be named - a spaniel with three legs (born so) with a litter of pups with four legs each.

From here we returned to have a ramble on Calton Hill and retired to our lodgings believing we had seen most of the sights of Edinburgh.

September 15 1850 : Sunday. Never having seen the Mass celebrated we this morning attend Roman Catholic Chapel. Having entered and being about to sit down we are asked for our tickets and are sent out again to get them. 3d each is asked which I rather grudgingly pay, and we are seated. Mass commences, but I could learn little from what I saw and not much more from the preacher, who was rather inaudible. The ceremonial was rather splendid and the music first rate. After dinner we were directed to St George's church to hear the celebrated Dr Candlish, but instead of going to the St George's Free church we got to St George's of the Established Church of Scotland, and in the evening we attended service in a concert room but of what particular denomination I don't know. The different sects - Established Churches, Free Churches and Presbyterian Churches - puzzled me sadly. In the two Protestant churches or congregations above attended I found the following peculiarities :- alms dishes placed on little tables, the tables covered with a clean white cloth, in the entrance; no organ or instrument of music is used, but the singing is led by a man termed, I believe, the Precentor. During the singing the congregation sit, during the Prayer, which in both cases was extempore, the people stand. A version of psalms and a collection of paraphrases and sanctuses I found bound up at the end of most or all the Bibles I saw in Scotland and which were sung at both places of worship. After the afternoon service we had a walk round the foot of the Castle, past Heriot's Hospital, down the Meadow Walk and through St George's Square once the abode of aristocracy, and Sir W. Scott having passed some of his youthful days in it make it memorable, but fashion and rank have left the old for the new town. There are several episcopal chapels or churches in Edinburgh but we did not attend any of them.

September 16 1850 : After an early breakfast we start at 7 o'clock for Glasgow which we reach after a two hours' ride. From the station we cross Glasgow on foot. As we pass along we skirt St George's Square from the centre of which rises a column crowned by a statue of Sir R. Peel and on a pedestal is a seated figure of James Watt. A little further on we pass the Exchange in front of which is an equestrian statue of the Duke of Wellington. We then turn into a street for breadth, traffic and general appearance more like the streets of London than any I have seen. In this street we looked up an arcade of great length. Having crossed this street and another square we at length reach the Broomielaw and embark on a steamer with two funnels. The banks of the Clyde present very many objects of interest, the clang of hammers at the iron shipbuilding yards being amongst the most striking. On reaching Bowling, a distance of eleven miles from Glasgow, we disembark and proceed to the Dumbartonshire Railway, and now we begin to feel our first little inconvenience. The carriages are all crowded and we crowd in whilst others follow. At every station we take up more passengers until we reach Balloch Fair which we see in the distance. All our rough customers depart and we make the rest of the journey in quiet. With my head out of the window I approach Loch Lomond. What a sight! So unlike anything I have ever seen before - the glassy smoothness of the water, the beauty of the islands upon it, the pretty banks that surround it, the silent majesty of the mountains beyond it - what a picture and how favoured we are - a clear atmosphere and brilliant sun. We alight on a wharf from the railway carriage and step into as respectable a steamer as ever I saw. Aft of the engine is a very elegant cabin and private rooms, and forward another large cabin devoted to gastronomic exercises, and as travelling has sharpened our appetites a five penny bottle of ale and an eight penny plate of cheese and bread disappear before us like a lot of vagrants before a policeman. The steamer threads amongst the islands - every turn brings us new scenery. As we begin at the bottom of the lake the shores are tame and pastoral, but as we proceed the scene changes. The pretty seat or mansion is changed for the little white-washed, one storey high cottage with its little potato patch or field of corn or meadow bearing strict contrast with the wild uncultivated hills around. The scene becomes more and more rugged, mountain after mountain appears in sight - at last Ben Lomond. The loch grows narrower. We pass Rob Roy's rock and cave, a beauteous waterfall falling into the lake, and then after a time we reach the head of the lake. We had hardly seen the head of the steamer turned round before there was a general move to the cabin and soon we had smoking hot before us roast beef, boiled beef, boiled mutton, potatoes etc. and after this we had a second taste of their cheese. We then went on deck again, and on arriving at the bottom of the lake we had to wait some time before the train was sent for us. That awkward fair is to blame for it. On getting into the railway carriage we manage well until we arrive at Balloch. A drunken man attempts our carriage but is successfully repulsed, Not so two women and a girl and infant. They force in, sadly against our will, and the woman with the infant and the lady with the infant of our party get up a quarrel and treat one another to a little tongue. When we reach Bowling a steamer is waiting for us but unfortunately it is not the steamer we ought to have gone by and here we have another long wait, and it is quite dark. Fears too begin to rise that we shall miss the train to Edinburgh. Other trains arrive, the boat fills with passengers, and at length we start but not before I have been assured that it is the slowest boat on the river and we shall have a long voyage.

At length however the Broomielaw is gained and we make all haste to the station which we reach at ten pm instead of half past eight. The trains are gone and the gates locked so we turn into Glasgow again and at Wilson's Temperance Hotel, corner of George's Square, we get a comfortable tea and lodgings …

In passing through Glasgow in the morning the fog was very dense but tonight, lit up, the streets look better. The hotel we stayed at was three storeys from the ground and was approached by a spiral staircase of stone. The rooms were well furnished and lighted - gas in the passages, staircase and bedrooms. We ordered tea and ham. The latter article I dispensed. Such a stack for a party of six I never saw [four other people had also missed their train] and to have seen the bread, cut thick without butter, you might have thought it was for six ploughmen. I joked about the ham and then served it out and by the time we had done, it was all done too. Evidently the landlady knew what sort of appetites Loch Lomond had given us better than we did. We got to rest after midnight and about six next morning, the **17th**, we are up and dressed, and without breakfast we travel to Edinburgh. The people at No.10 seem delighted to see us, the chambermaid comes skipping down looking quite pleased. They are so glad, they thought some accident had befallen us. Really it is pleasing to find strangers thus interested in us.

Now then look quick - the bill and breakfast. We must be off again in less than an hour. We had all packed up, very soon breakfast is despatched and bill paid. We took parting glances at the Castle, Arthur's Seat and other points as we left the city, and in spite of the haste and the excitement that was to follow there was a slight tinge of sadness mingled in my last looks on the beautiful city of Edinburgh. We had spent some happy days in it, the precursors of a long length of happy days I trust to be spent in usefulness to society and the fear of God. Many are the peculiarities that strike the stranger during his sojourn in Edinburgh, not the least is the number of bell pulls on each side of some doors and the construction that leads to it. Our lodging may serve as an example. Fronting the street it displayed two shops, one approached by descending a few steps and was a gutta-percha depot; above this was a music shop approached by a few steps upwards from the street leading into a passage; direct in front on entering you perceive the door leading to the offices of Macpherson and Syme, printers; turning to the left you have the entrance of the music shop and directly opposite the staircase. Ascend this and you reach the dining and sitting rooms of the hotel, but if you require to go into your bedroom you must mount the common stair again, when at the next landing you find three front doors. At the one of Sinclair's you knock and the door is opened to you by the maid. There were several lodging rooms on this floor but we had to mount another flight to No.9. We never could get from our sitting room to our lodging room without knocking at the door upstairs. It appeared like two different establishments.

[The account of the couple's return to Ripon is contained in section 1 on the Family.]

11. PEOPLE

The only uniting theme in this set of extracts is that they are all about individual people.

July 7 1842 : **John Lancaster** of Thirsk, a schoolfellow, came over today. He has been at sea for the last eight years. For the last four years he has never been in England, being in the Mediterranean partly in the Merchants' and partly in the Queen's Service and lately in the Royal Yacht Squadron. He was present at the siege of Jean de Acre. Since, he has swum the Bosphorous, visited Greece and Italy etc. having command of a yacht, the owner of the vessel taking the tour.

December 7 1842 : **John Tuting** and **John Blacker** set out for Portsmouth by the Mail to York and then by railway. They arc both going to enter the Royal Navy. John Tuting has completed his apprenticeship as a grocer but nothing but the sea will suit him now.

March 27 1843 : John Tuting calls upon me. He arrived from London yesterday. He has procured a situation in York. He gives the men of the Royal Navy a very bad name for swearing etc. His situation was a Boy and his chief duty to wash the decks and other such jobs and to pull the jolly boat to and from the ship to land. The ship he was aboard was the *Victory.* There is a small brass plate let into the deck on which is inscribed 'Here Nelson fell'. The *Victory* is not seaworthy but constantly at anchor divested of the greater part of her rigging and guns and used as a guard ship on which sailors are trained (126).

February 22 1843 : Today a daring character, **Elijah Sinkler**, is captured near Pateley Bridge in the Township of Fountains Earth. Sinkler is examined and committed to York Castle for attempting the life of the gamekeeper who captured him. Sinkler, it appears, about ten years ago was transported for life, though he was sentenced to be executed, he having poached and committed felony and when taken by our police was rescued by his brother and another who cut and maimed them before they let him go. After he was transported his brother behaved better. Many were the attempts made to capture him, but in vain. About a twelve month ago Elijah returned, having escaped, and was left unmolested in his native place until he again resumed his former lawless life. He and his brother Jack, encamped upon the moor, shot what they liked and where they liked until he was captured on Tuesday by Robinson, gamekeeper to J. Yorke Esqr. and two of his assistants. Robinson knocked him down with a stick or Sinkler would have shot him presenting a pistol which was loadened with ball.

Sinkler behaved in a very impudent manner to the magistrates. When asked his trade he said it was to kill all the game he could and other sayings much worse.

February 23 1843 : Sinkler is taken on the Mail to York heavily ironed. He told the mob he was sure to come back as snow and rain falls. He called for cheers and I am sorry to write they were given. It speaks very little for the loyalty of my townsmen, especially the lower order, who pity him and inveigh against those who captured him. Indeed they defend him in all he has done. The other brother still keeps aloof and cannot be taken.

March 30 1843 : John Sinkler, the brother of the outlaw who was mentioned in my journal before, was brought to Ripon in custody and sent to York Castle. His brother Elisha has been transported (127).

January 25 1844 : **George Wharton** whom I visited [October 1842] was this day interred in Kirkby Malzeard Churchyard aged about 114 years. For a fuller account see **Miscellany.**

From **Miscellany** 1844 : The man whose name stands at the head of this page was born in London. The only circumstance he told of his childhood in his latter days was his being present along with his mother at the opening of the first Wesleyan chapel in London, when John Wesley preached. The chapel had been formed out of an iron foundry. His life had been much chequered with good and evil. He had been impressed and served on board a man-of-war for many years. He had served at the taking of Quebec. He never told the name of his ship. He had no pension nor would he ever say why or how he left the service of his country although he never failed to tell that he was pressed to sea against his will. The villagers will have it he ran away. He came to Laverton and was married to a woman of a small income. He took up the business of a weaver (for in those days every dame spun her own cloth and it went to the next village to be woven). He was a great friend of my mother's uncle (with whom my mother was brought up) who was also a weaver.

George Wharton had one son who attained manhood, became an exciseman and died. After he became a widower and childless he still continued to live on the banks of the Laver upon his little income. In October 1842 I visited his cot. It was the Feast and he had been that day dining with the Oddfellows. (He always took the chair on such occasions; he dined with all the various lodges for some years, said grace, recited a piece or sung a song.) To his last days he walked about the village, smoked his pipe and took his glass of ale. He retained his mental faculties to the last. He bought some little property when he was younger and sold it a year or two before his death. He signed his name very well without the aid of glasses. He made a very many wills. The autograph at the head of this article [omitted] is supposed to have been cut off one of them. The words behind the signature bear out the idea. The signature was given me by his neighbour, Mr Shaw.

At length old George outlived all his property and money except the income which he could not dispose of it being entailed. He therefore, the income being too small for him, gave into the hands of the next heir agreeing that he should keep him for the rest of his life. This man removed old George from Laverton to Moorhouses near Masham. A few weeks after, the poor old man died, and on 25th January 1844 his remains were interred in Kirkby Malzeard churchyard. No one could ascertain his exact age. His register had been sought in all the parish churches in London without success. His age was supposed to be about 114 years. He might have lived, there is no doubt, a few years longer had he been suffered to remain in the valley in which he had dwelt so long. In religion he was a follower of Wesley and was at one time a local preacher. He hoped he was also a follower of Christ and that now after his long sojourn in this vale of tears he had found rest (128).

April 10 1844 : In my morning walk overtook **Mr Brown**, druggist [John Brown had a shop in Westgate]. We entered into conversation on Botany. He told me he was going to Red Bank for a very scarce plant. I told him that the other day I brought in two flowers. One I found out to be anemone; the other I could not tell what it was. I described it and it proved to be the very plant he was now in search of. It is called the Yellow Star of Bethlehem, a small yellow flower now in bloom. Its petals are sharp-pointed and are about six in number. The plant is nowhere to be found near Ripon except in the part of Red Bank near Gibraltar [near the junction of Whitcliffe and Hell Wath lanes]. The plants Mr Brown was going to procure were for a gent. in Lancashire. Mr Brown has collected and preserved in a herbarium no less than 300 specimens of distinct species of flowers. Land shells are now his study of which he already possesses 80 specimens. Mr Fletcher (founder of Green Royd) (86) and my mother thus account for so many and scarce flowers being found in Red Bank. The River Skell which flows along Red Bank flows also under the Abbey and through the gardens of Fountains. This little river frequently overflows and it is possible, nay probable, that roots have been from time to time washed down the river from thence and found a resting place in the flats where they may now grow. Sure it is a romantic thought. I am now gathering flowers from roots which the holy fathers of Fountains brought into this neighbourhood and planted in their own retreat.

November 3 1844 : **John Addison**, our neighbour, is interred in the Cathedral burying ground. He died on the 31st of last month aged 72. At the same time John Burgess Skipsey was also interred. He had been in high office as an Odd fellow. 400 of that fraternity accompanied his remains to the grave. He having been a bell-ringer, a dumb peal was rung; for some years he was journeyman to Mrs Gowing (2).

April 10 1845 : **William Harrison** died aged 85. He was a relation by marriage, having married my father's aunt.
April 13 1845 : Mr Harrison is buried. He had been a singing man for 50 years at the Cathedral and lately received a pension from the Cathedral revenues. He was met at the West door by the Choir, was sung before him up the Nave etc. Formerly it was usual to sing any person belonging to the Choir through the streets from the house but this has been abolished.

From the **Miscellany 1845** on **Mrs Lawrence** of Studley Royal. This lady, whose death occurred on 30th July, was the greatest friend to the poor which we had in our neighbourhood. Not only the poor but the middle and higher ranks of society greatly respected her, and never I believe did the death of any one cause more

Plate 15. Portrait of Mrs Lawrence of Studley Royal.

sorrow to the people of Ripon than did the death of this amiable lady. The funeral at her own request was attended with as little pomp as possible but as the enclosed programme [omitted] will show, this did not deter the inhabitants from paying her remains the only mark of respect that was left them to show. The programmes were printed by us and the people showed great anxiety to obtain them in order to preserve them or send them to distant relatives ... Her long life was unmarked by any striking events. She lived temperately and of late years never remained a night from her own hall. Yet her seat was oft well-filled with company, whom she continued to receive until her last illness.

She gave largely to the societies established by our Church for the bettering of our race and for leading men to God. She has contributed largely to every local good work, built churches, established schools, given away books and, in fine, her liberality has taken almost every form which Christian charity could devise. Although possessed of a princely income she suffered it not to accumulate, such was her benevolence.

Formerly she used to ride about her park and grounds upon an ass and the first time I saw her it was near her house leading her ass. I was with my father, mother and sister. She patted me on the cheek and talked to me. Her care of Fountains Abbey has been all that an antiquarian could wish. Many things have been done to keep it from going into more decay and everything has been done judiciously.

August 10 1845 : [the Sunday shortly after Mrs Lawrence's funeral which took place at Kirkby Fleetham and not at Ripon.] The Cathedral pulpit and the hangings in the Choir are all covered with black cloth. The Corporation attend church this morning in their robes, the mace etc. covered with crepe. The Bishop preached a funeral sermon.

October 26 1846 : A week or more ago a large tablet has been erected to **Capt. Elliott** in the Cathedral. The Captain had circumnavigated the globe under Capt. Cook and had been wounded in action under Lord Rodney as the tablet duly chronicles. He was born near Ripon, entered the Royal Navy, got wounded and then a pension, got married and then a family and built the house known as Elliott House [now Holmefield House]. I remember him well. He wore peculiar clothes, had a pigtail and powdered hair.

January 3 1847 : Tonight Mr Whiteside (25) in his discourse alluded to the death of **John Wray**, the Sexton ... John Wray is the last of the officers of the church who ministered in the church when it was opened. Since that time - 1827 - he has had the care of the buildings. During thirteen years of his early life he served in the Royal Navy, was in several actions and has been wounded. He served on board the *Revenge* at the battle of Trafalgar. After this he returned to his native place.

December 1847 : On 8th December, at his chambers in the Albany, London, **Sir Charles Dalbiac** died. Sir Charles was a man well known at Ripon in consequence of his connexion with the Daltons, he having married one of Col. Dalton's daughters, but he owes the greater part of his fame in consequence of his being a candidate of the Conservative interest in the contested election of 1832. At that time he was unsuccessful but he served in two Parliaments for Ripon after that. Sir Charles was born 1776. In 1793 he joined 4th Dragoons, when he took the lowest station of an officer. He died Colonel of the Regiment. He rose gradually from a cornet to that office. He never served with any other regiment but this. He fought with them in the Peninsula and on the plains of India. He was knighted in 1831. Sir Charles leaves one child behind him - the Duchess of Roxburgh.

February 21 1849 : Today at the University of Dublin **Mr Whiteside**, late Incumbent of Trinity Church, preaches a Latin sermon and has the degree of D.D. conferred upon him.

June 5 1849 : **Haseldine Sharpin**, an old schoolfellow of mine, is presented with a life member's ticket at the Institute for his services. He leaves Ripon for Australia next morning.

January 26 1851 : **Mr Smith** of Malton, formerly Master of Jepson's Hospital and my schoolmaster, lectures at the Institute on 'Happiness' ... the Hon. Secretary, the Treasurer, and two of the committee members at least were pupils of his. When Mr Smith was at Ripon, besides being Master of the Hospital, he had a good school including some boarders, and the greatest part of the sons of the respectable tradesmen of the town. Mr S. is now manager of the City and County Bank at Malton. He has turned vegetarian and a work entitled **Fruits and Farinacea** is the fruit of his pen.

May 30 1851 : **John Robinson**, formerly a basket maker with old Tommy Daniel, was buried. He met with an accident while engaged with a cartload of willows in the gateway leading to Precious basket maker's shop [now the Wakeman's House] near our house .

June 18 1852 : Today I attend the funeral of **Mr Joseph Barker**, Artist. I first made acquaintance with Mr Barker in London at Horsman's. He was then a skilful portrait painter. Since that time however he has risen much in fame. His painting may be judged of from his picture of Dr Paley hung in the Dispensary here. He married Alice Tuting by whom he leaves surviving children.

12. MISCELLANEOUS EVENTS

This section contains a number of extracts, some long, some short, which do not fit comfortably elsewhere.

May 14 1838 : After tea took a walk to the aqueduct on the River Laver. The aqueduct is situated not very far above Bishopton Bridge. The water by means of a dam thrown across the river is directed into an artificial channel through which it runs to Bishopton Mill which it supplies with water. The natural bed of the Laver crosses the artificial channel. Being a great deal higher than the natural bed it is carried across the Laver by means of an aqueduct constructed of wood.

April 27 1842: Was awakened this morning by an accident. Mr Coldeck and others on their way to Boro'bridge from Grewelthorpe in a cart ran the shafts of the vehicle they were in into our shop window by which two shutters and two panes of glass were broken. The pony was no worse. It happened about 6 o'clock.

May 17 1842 : The Order of the Peaceful Doves (129) with a band of music at their head paraded the streets after being at the Minster where they had a sermon by the Revd R. Poole. At night the Doves were anything but peaceful and their band disturbed the inhabitants by beating their drum in a very boisterous manner [until] about one o'clock in the morning.

December 7 1842 : Some portrait painters having come into the town lately the apprentices etc. in Mr Harrison's office (21) have subscribed and had the likeness of the oldest apprentice taken, upon which the following lines have been written :
    Mayster Hodgson - Anno Aetatis XVIII, D'm MDCCCXLII
    Typographers draw nigh and look on one
    The like to whom ye never more shall see,
    Apprentice chief to Mayster Harrison
    But he the smallest of those children be.
    O Hodgson, depictured here thou standeth
    With 'well cast roller' by thy 'inky stone'
    A fit example thou wilt always be
    To future 'devylles' of the 'presse and forme'.
    Auton and Jones excel thee in thy strength,
    Proctour in comely face and flowing haire,
    Joseph in mischief-making - George in cunning
    Rodney and Jackson in uncorking beer;
    Powell the prince of smokers too
    In 'arrangements final' shirking
    But none exceed thee in thy honestie,
    Thy patience, willingnesse and veritie (130).   Sic ecrivit J. R. W.

The portrait is admirably drawn. Mayster Hodgson is in the working dress with apron and a 'well cast roller' in his hand.

March 17 1843 : [At Galphay] we met with an old man aged 78 - John Newbald. He knew my grandmother (mother's side). He said "We (that is my grandmother and he) were both Nitherdale born 'uns". He remembers coming to Ripon quite a boy when there were only three shops in the Market Place.

April 14 1843 : Tonight the Bellman has announced that the fare by the *Garter* coach to Thirsk is 1/- each person inside or out. This is caused by Mr Jones (late the Bishop's coachman) of the **Star** Inn commencing a coach called the *Star* from Ripon to Thirsk, fares 2/- and 1/6; before this week the fares of the Mail have been 2/6 and 3/6 (131). So the *Star* and *Garter* are now in opposition. Pawson, the owner of the Mail, commenced his opposition coach, the *Garter*, the same day (last Monday) as Jones commenced his, in hopes to run it off the road.

September 18 1843 : Today labourers commence to pull down the **Lamb** Inn, Skellgate. It is a very old house - the bedsteads are quite curiosities and are built in with the house.

December 29 1843 : Henry Browne [Thirlway apprentice] did not sleep at home tonight. The Peaceful Doves (129) had a ball and tea. Mr Sayers [landlord of the **Coach and Horses** in Westgate] provided, and Henry was employed by Mr S. as tickettaker. The ball was held in the Public Rooms (40). The party although composed of the lower classes behaved in a more respectable manner than many their superiors do at a higher ball.

Miscellany 1843 : My sister in reading a book called 'The Manners and Customs of all Nations' found an account of a 'Curious Custom practised at Ripon in Yorkshire' which is as follows. When a family removes from one house to another or when a newcomer enters his house, a table is spread before his door on which is placed bread, cheese and ale. And if the master be of ability he asks his neighbours to supper.

On seeing this I began to make enquiries had it been so, for no such practise is now observed. My father says it was, and the table was spread on the Midsummer Eve after the party had entered the house. On one occasion he remembers seeing it in front of the **Royal Oak** Inn in Kirkgate. My mother once saw a table spread in like manner in Blossomgate when she was quite young.

It was customary in olden times at Kirkby Malzeard for a certain number of young women to precede the coffin at the funeral of one of their sex and age, bearing a garland of white paper and a white glove which after the funeral was suspended in the church. My mother remembers seeing gloves and garlands so suspended in memory of young who had died.

January 6 1844 : Miss Sergeantson enquires at our shop for a parcel. None had come. On application at the **Unicorn** Inn, Boots said he had left it at our shop on the evening of January 2nd (132).

January 8 1844 : More enquiries about the parcel which contained a gold chain five yards long and an eye glass.

January 10 1844 : Boots was summoned to the Court House and father, sister and I were sent for when we were examined before Mr Oxley Esqr. and Dr Paley. Boots said that on receiving the parcel he carried it to Mr Thirlway's shop when Miss Thirlway and Mr Thirlway Junr received it and paid him 10d carriage and 2d postage, and one of them signed the book.

Sister said that the 2nd of January being a washing day she was never in the shop all evening.

Mr T. Junr said he was in the shop the greater part of the evening but he never saw Boots. Was ready to swear the writing in the book was not his nor yet his sister's.

Mr T. Senr said he never was absent the whole of the evening and therefore the parcel could not have been brought in without his knowledge, although Boots had said that Mr T. was not in the shop. The whole four were ready to swear what they had said.

Boots than entered into a recognizance of £10 and Mr Robinson of the Inn in another £10 for his appearance at a future time.

Numerous rumours were afloat that we had lost or stolen it. It caused us much trouble and anxiety.

January 12 1844 : Mr Fisher, High Skellgate [the brewer ?], brought the parcel to our shop, but took it home again until Miss Sergeantson called at his house for it. Boots had left it at his house on the evening in question it being directed to be left at Mr Fisher's ... Boots on the same morning appeared at the Court House to be released from his recognizance. Mr Oxley reprimanded him, and told him that had he sworn all that he had said he put it in the power of Messrs Thirlway to transport him.

Thus ended an affair which caused me much trouble and uneasiness but which has learnt me a lesson - may the impression grow deeper and stronger. It is this, trust not that a good name will have great weight with the world when you are doubted or in misfortune, neither be too anxious for the favour of men, but seek rather the fear of the Lord. He is a friend indeed.

June 7 1844 : In the afternoon an alarm was given. The boiling house at the Paddock Varnish Works (R. Williamson & Co.) had caught fire on account of the quantity of varnish, turpentine etc. which the building contained. It [the fire] was soon contained by the great exertions which were made by the people who flocked to the place. The fire was prevented from spreading to either of the adjoining buildings, one the dwelling house of C. Williamson and on the other side the warehouses etc. One of the engines arrived on the ground but never played on the building.

June 27 1844 : Today an accident at our corner in consequence of a careless fellow leaving two horses and carts ladened with corn to turn the corner by themselves. The last cart got upon the flags and the wheel was stopped only by coming into contact with the window frame. Luckily no squares were broken but the woodwork was damaged.

June 28 1844 : Another accident. A carriage full of ladies started from the *Unicorn* which being furiously driven the horses could not turn the corner of Skellgate but ran the carriage against the Yorkshire Bank (133). The pole was splintered to pieces, but the door being lined with iron is little worse.

Miscellany 1844 : In the month of March of the present year alterations were made at the [Borrage] Well (134) which brought it to my notice. Having known this well ever since I was a little child I now for my own amusement pen its history.

When first I sipped the waters of this well, the land around was waste. There were no gardens, no houses on Borrage, but instead a bare pasture and heaps of rubbish. The well was then on a level with the field and surrounded with a wooden railing; the covering, which yet remains, is a stone fashioned not unlike a niche, the water flowing in and out at the bottom. Inside and near the top it bears the following inscription - "Utilitate Publica, AD MDCCLVIII". An old iron dish hung on one side for the use of the passer-by. Thus it was in olden times.

But at length the land was enclosed and Mr Nowell, after he had built Trinity Church, erected four houses very near the old well which are now known as Borrage Terrace or South Parade. The well was enclosed in the gardens and the poor old stone was well nigh buried in mould. Instead of the old well a pump was erected close by the roadside as it was illegal to deprive the public of the use of the spring. The new pump was erected at Mr Nowell's expense who agreed also to keep it in repair. This was done in 1827. Upon the front of the little building was the following inscription - "1827 James Britain Esqr., Mayor".

Mischievous people very soon and very often damaged and broke the pump, until at length Mr Nowell grew weary of repairing it. The pump was broken and consequently the public were deprived of their right until the spring of this year, when the Board of Highways had the well again thrown open, the pump cleared away and the building which sheltered it became an entrance to the old well to which steps had been laid down and around which iron rails had been erected, and on the side of which a dish suspended to a chain is now fixed. The inscription also over the building, which had no right there as neither the Mayor (James Britain, Brewer) nor the Corporation had anything to do with it, was erased and the following cut out instead :- "This well was given for the use of the public by W. Richardson Esqr., 1758".

I am sorry to say that the Board of Highways had fault found with them for thus restoring the well. For one I regret not the expense, but am glad it has been done.

April 4 1845 : On Easter Tuesday the new fire engine was first played in the Market Place. It has been purchased by subscriptions collected by Mr S. Tutin during his mayoralty (135). It has two pipes and it can be made to throw two streams of water at one time. It is of power much superior to the old one.

August 11 1845 : During last month Mr Blakeborough, clock and watch maker in the Middle Street, has put out a large clock face over his door, and on Friday last he made an addition to it in the shape of a little wooden figure which strikes the hours upon a bell.

September 19 1845 : Today Ralph Gowing's apprenticeship expired (2). He had supper at Dixon Gatenby's [*Lamb and Flag,* High Skellgate] to which I was invited. The evening was spent in a very jovial manner. We had a many songs, a game at Simon and a Salt and Sawdust (136). Left the company at five. Many of them did not break up until after breakfast which they had at Mrs Gowing's.

December 4 1845 : Today at noon an alarm of fire was given in Westgate, a building behind Mr Farrar's being on fire. In the top room which is the schoolroom (137), a fire is kept. It is supposed that a hot cinder had fallen through by some means into the lower room which was filled with apples, potatoes, straw, empty hampers and lumber. Below this was the wine and spirit vaults. The fire commenced among the straw. Alarm being given the engines were brought to the place and the spirits and wine were removed by plenty of willing hands. The fire was soon put down after the new engine was brought into play - about £20 or £30 damage has been done. Credit is due to the inhabitants for their activity and the engine did its work well. It is the first fire it has been at. The building is of three stories. The fire did not reach the roof.

April 1 1847 : Today a wagon ladened with corn belonging to Winksley, Skara Mill, overturned a cart ladened with guano belonging to Mr Pearson of Melmerby on to our shop window looking into Skellgate. The cart broke neither framework nor glass but a bag of guano shattered one square only. It is wonderful that so little damage was done.

November 13 1848 : At seven o'clock the alarm bell was rung violently upon which I hastened into the street. The report was that some stacks near to Norton Conyers (138) were on fire. This report was soon changed to "Norton Conyers is on fire". The engines were got out with speed. First went the old engine under the care of Mr Daniel. This was drawn by an old cart horse. Then followed another old engine under the management of Ralph Gowing, who in his haste got the first animal yoked he could find and that was his own pony. These were shortly followed by the new and powerful engine under the care of Mr Lambert (139). No light from the conflagration could be seen from the outskirts of the town and some doubted the truth of the report. Many persons set off in breathless haste and some got to the gates of the park before the engines. The engines too were ladened with as many men as could find room to cling to them.

People who did not follow the engines said the two first would never reach the top of Hutton Bank, but somehow the first got up first and when Ralph Gowing arrived at the hill and found it lately laid with new stones the men got off the engine, lifted it upon the footpath and so it easily pulled up the hill, proving that where there is a will there is a way. The next engine that came to the hill though drawn by four post horses with postillions stuck fast, and the traces broke. Thus giving another instance that the race is not always to the swift. The first engine that arrived was Daniel's, closely followed by Ralph. At the gates they were met by

Collinson, the head policeman, who had preceded them and gone up to the mansion. There was no fire. The report was false. The engines then turned round. The other engine then came up and it too was turned back. It is supposed the report originated through some passengers in the railway train having seen a great fire which had been made to consume ... brushwood near the place. The night was very windy and it blew the flames about a great deal.

June 24 1850 : The foundation stone of a new dispensary (140) was laid down by Dr Paley (141). The site has been given by Earl de Grey [Mrs Lawrence's heir at Studley] and the building will be erected with a legacy left to the institution by Mrs Lawrence.

August 28 1850 : A meeting earlier had agreed to a testimonial to Dr Paley for his services re the dispensary. It was agreed upon that a portrait of the worthy doctor should be painted to hang in the hall of the new building. The subscription already exceeds £100 and today Mr Barker (142) has been chosen out of a number of competitors to paint the picture. Mr B. has been exhibiting a portrait of Canon Wray of Manchester at his brother-in-law's, John Tuting, for some time past. The picture is a really good one and is much admired ... The new dispensary rises fast and when finished will be the most ornamental modern building in the city.

April 14 1851 : The beautiful glass chandelier in the Town Hall has been removed and tonight for the first time I have seen the different rooms lit with gas. No public occasion - they were lit for trial.

April 13 1852 : At the Cathedral Chapter the first public step was taken towards a new stained glass window for the east window of the Cathedral to commemorate the creation of the See and its first Bishop (22). The total cost is estimated at about £1,200. The diocese is to be divided into seven districts for the purpose of collecting subscriptions etc. The greater part of it is already stained - three compartments were exhibited in the Crystal Palace last year.

All the remaining items in this section deal with the **GAS WORKS** (143)

May 7 1842 : Called at the Gas Works. They are getting new retorts.

May 21 1844 : The gasometer at the Gas Works being too small, the shareholders have come to a determination of erecting another which will be larger and on a more improved principle, and to repair the old one. For this purpose they intend to devote the dividends instead of receiving them themselves until the expense is paid. Mr Malam of Thirsk has contracted for the erecting of it for [a blank space follows].

For some days back workmen have been digging out the tank. Today Mr Malam, nephew to the contractor, commences superintending the work.

Mr Malam is proprietor of the Knaresbro', Thirsk and other Gas Works. He has lately obtained a contract for new gas works, pipes, lamps etc. at Hamburg to replace those burnt at the late fire. Frenchmen, Germans and others sent in estimates but failed to obtain it.

May 24 1844 : The works at the Gas House go on very slowly the gravel which they are digging out being loose and abounding with springs. They have dug through the gravel and reached the clay underneath. The hole is 9 feet deep.

June 1 1844 : Mr Malam after staying a week at Ripon returned to Thirsk. The foundation stones are laid and more than half of the brickwork built.

June 8 1844 : The brickwork for the gasometer is now finished except the bottom or floor which is to be bedded with clay, laid with bricks and strongly cemented.

August 12 1847 : Attended a meeting of the Gas Proprietors at the Gas Works to receive the report of Mr [name omitted], a gentleman who has been inspecting the works for the purpose of having them remodelled. He recommends a new hydraulic main, placed in a better position, a new washer, more condensing pipes, a larger purifying apparatus, a meter, alterations to the hanging of both the gasometers and a governor. His improvements were agreed to. This is the first meeting I have attended.

November 5 1847 : Today Robert Vest and his sons receive their dismissal from the Gas House and new hands commence making gas.

January 7 1848 : The three workmen from London finish for the present at the Gas Works tonight. They have erected a new hydraulic main but which is not yet in use, new condensers, scrubber, pumpers, station meter and governor, all of which are in operation.

November 9 1848 : This evening the Gas Company treat their workpeople and those who have assisted in making the alterations which are now completed with a supper. About 20 sat down. The company consists of Matthew Coates, Chairman, Mr Trees, Vice-Chairman, the lamp-lighters, bricklayers, labourers, carters etc. who filled up each side of the table. The supper consisted of beef roasted and boiled, leg of mutton, rabbit pie, apple pie and ale. About half after eight they were joined by Messrs Snowden, Thirlway, C. Horn, W. Judson, H. Stevenson Junr and myself. The party were then drinking ale, smoking tobacco and looking as sober as judges. I was much surprised to find the supper and entertainment took place in the Retort House, which has been enlarged. The walls have been whitewashed and everything else painted with gas tar. The walls were ornamented with evergreens and paper white and red roses. Everything looked clean, neat and comfortable. On being accommodated with seats we produced four bottles of gin. The ale was cleared away and gin and water became the going articles. Mr Snowden proposed the health of Matthew Coates … Mr Horn proposed Mr Snowden. Mr Snowden returned thanks and proposed 'The Ladies' as several of their wives had stolen in to hear the fun. I returned thanks and proposed Mr Horn. Mr Snowden proposed 'The Mayor and Corporation'. Mr Horn responded to both. The speeches were relieved by songs. Mr Thirlway led off and called upon Mr Daniel. Mr D. sang and called upon me. I sang and called upon Mrs Abbott and next her children sang 'Mary Blane'. We left the works at a quarter past ten after ordering three bottles of gin.

January 17 1851 : In my walk I saw the work now going on under the care of Ralph Gowing, who is laying down gas pipes to light four more lamps from North Street to the station.

13. MARY JANE'S DIARY.

Mary Jane Thirlway was the younger daughter of Henry Steel Thirlway. In March 1874, at the age of sixteen, she followed her father's example and began to keep a diary, despite her brother's prophecy that she "would not write in it more than once a year". At that time the family at Thirlway's Corner consisted of her father and mother, her brother, Henry Mann Thirlway, born in 1851, and Mary Jane herself, born in 1858. Mary Jane's elder sister, called Alice Ann after her mother, had died six years earlier. There is evidence that the household also included a maidservant.

When the diary opens Mary Jane was still at school. She attended a private girls' school run by Mrs Alice Barker in Park Street, a school which seems to have taken both day and boarding pupils. Apart from Mrs Barker, whose name is mentioned in connection with a school expedition to Brimham Rocks, the only teachers referred to in the diary are those who taught foreign languages. The earliest of these, a Frenchman, and the second, a German, were shared with the private boys' boarding school at Bishopton Close to the west of Ripon but when the headmaster of that school, Mr William Fowler Stephenson, died, and his school had to close, Mrs Barker procured the services of the Frenchman teaching at Ripon Grammar School (144). Of the German Mary Jane wrote "He was very nice, so kind and timid". When she had met the second French master she recorded that he was "not such a petit maitre as the last Frenchman we had". Assuming she was using the expression 'petit maitre' correctly it would appear that the first French master was something of a dandy. The only other subject mentioned specifically in connection with school is singing which she says she only began half way through 1874, but she did not enjoy singing lessons "and cannot sing so well as when I am alone".

At the end of 1874 Mary Jane left school, an event she records in her diary with the words "I have finished my education. I am glad the examinations are over. It is such dreadful hard work but I passed them all - and got a beautiful book almost like the one Lizzie Askwith got". However she goes on to contradict the first part of this statement by declaring that she means "to work very hard at music, singing, French, Latin and history and such like" and vows "not to read so many novels if any". Unfortunately for her good intentions at the end of 1875 she feels she has wasted her first year after school and remarks on a growing tendency to get up late in the mornings. "When at school I used to get up at six at the latest even in winter. Now I only get down at breakfast time and sometimes after that." We are left wondering at what time the family had breakfast. So far as her studies are concerned she hopes that things will turn out better after the expected return to Ripon of her friend, Sarah Snow. For example they will be able to read French together. Sarah's return apparently had the anticipated good result because we read subsequently that Sarah has helped her with 'harmony' and that they have both joined with two other ladies to form a Latin class taught by Mr Aslin, a

Plate 16. Henry Steel Thirlway and his wife on the occasion of their 41st wedding anniversary, September 10th 1891. The younger woman standing at the back is probably Mary Jane, their daughter

relative of one of the others. Soon she also refers to taking music classes with a Mr Crow and resolves to practise two hours a day, at what exactly she does not say, although a reference to a visit of a piano-tuner may be relevant. Soon afterwards she joins the Musical Society where she sings contralto and reports that she very much enjoys the rehearsals. She has obviously got over her difficulty in singing in the presence of others. This interest in music may of course reflect her father's influence. His journal shows him to have had a great love of both vocal and instrumental music. And indeed her concern for continuing her education after leaving school reflects her father's keenness for continuous self-improvement for its own sake. There was no question in those days of girls in Mary Jane's position preparing for any career. The only work mentioned in the diary was strictly voluntary and usually connected with the church.

Church activities did indeed play an important role in the life of Mary Jane as they had done and were still doing in the life of her father. The very first entry in her diary contains a reference to her work as a Sunday School teacher which she took very seriously. "There is a prayer meeting for Sunday School teachers and District Visitors at the Church Institute tonight (145). I am going as I sadly want the Lord's help in teaching my class. I know so little of His love. My life is full of broken resolutions". In June 1875 she records "I am getting on better with my class now. Elizabeth Fleming has taken a turn for the better. She must have seen I thought her and Jane Trueman the black sheep of the flock". On a more mundane level she refers to dressing two dolls to raise funds for Sunday School treats which apparently were provided not only for the scholars but also extended to a tea for their parents at which she and Mama poured the tea. The teachers too had their excursion, on one occasion, with Trinity Choir, to Hackfall near Grewelthorpe (146) on which occasion she wrote rather scornfully of two newly engaged couples - one pair too young she thinks to be engaged - "and of course when we were coming home the engaged pairs were lost". She goes on to write, "We came home by moonlight. I enjoyed the drive as much as anything. We sang nearly all the way home." The diary contains references too to a garden party at the Bishop's Palace where after refreshments in the dining room they went into the chapel for an address by the Bishop, and to a journey with her father to Wath for the re-opening of the church and the dedication of a new peal of bells, after which they had luncheon at Norton Hall. Other church-related activities included helping with Band of Hope (147) teas and with church bazaars like the one held in January, 1877, to clear Trinity Church debts - "1½ days decorating and 3 days selling", she records, led to the raising of £250 after all expenses had been paid. At another bazaar in May 1879, at which she and a friend officiated at the refreshment stall, their stall raised a clear £82 towards funds for the Church Missionary Society and the Jews' Society. More regular activities were in connection with the working party for the Zenana Mission (148). This working party was set up in October 1875, and she reports that Mr A.T. Askwith asked her to keep the accounts. Her other contribution was leather work. The working party was still in action in June 1877, when she reports going out "with Mama collecting for the Birds Nest [sic] and begging remnants from the drapers for the Zenana working party. Mr Ebdell has just sent in a splendid parcel" (149).

Probably the highlight of Trinity Church activities during this period was the Jubilee celebrations held in November 1877, fifty years after Trinity was consecrated. At the end of the week she records, "On Sunday we had special sermons, on Monday a school treat, on Tuesday a parochial tea followed by speeches and music and on Wednesday a special service at eleven and a luncheon at 1 pm and a service at night again. Papa spoke on Monday and Tuesday nights and on Wednesday at the luncheon. He was called upon to respond to the toast of "the congregation". A subscription of £200 has been raised to defray the cost of the church yard being planted with trees and otherwise improved and to discharge the debt on the parsonage. The proceeds of the six collections is to be employed in mission work in Allhallowgate". The following year she writes of going to the Allhallowgate Mission Room where there was a branch of the Yorkshire Penny Bank run under church auspices by Mrs Goodier, wife of the vicar of Holy Trinity. Mrs Goodier and her husband were going to Switzerland for six weeks and Mary Jane and a Miss Evans were to have the care of the bank while they were away. The church seems to have placed great trust in this young woman (150).

Of course not all Mary Jane's activities were related to Holy Trinity Church. On March 26 1874, for example, she writes, "I did not go to Church last night. Lizzie Holley came to know if I would go with them to a Magic Lantern [sic] in the Temperance Hall on "The Drunkard's Life". There were also slides on phrenology and astronomy and some comic ones. Mr Fisher was showing it from near Thirsk where her [Lizzie's] cousins, Sam and J… are at school. I enjoyed it very much but I enjoyed more Sam's tales of school" (151). She also that year enjoyed going to a Dog Show after which she writes, "Watch had the impudence to fly at the largest dog that could have eaten Watch at two bites". Later that day she went to Mr Snow's to play croquet. "We played until it was quite dark and then Harry brought a lamp and we played by lamplight".

A week after the croquet game she is making preparations for her attendance at the annual Mayor's Picnic. She is to wear a white muslin dress "with four flounces … so it will take some goffering". The "Picnic" was held on July 16th in Studley Park. "There were 240 there", she writes, "mostly of the upper class. We had a beautiful day. The luncheon was at two o'clock. We had it in a marquee in the park. The mayor met us all at the entrance of the tent which was curtained off from the rest as a reception room. Then we went in to luncheon. The tables were splendidly set out. There was almost every delicacy possible including iced champagne. After luncheon there were numerous toasts and then we wandered about the Abbey and grounds until about half past five when there was dancing until seven when we had tea". After tea there was more dancing and they came home about nine. Some picnic!

Other less unusual excursions mentioned are visits to Clotherholme, Mackershaw and Aldfield woods to gather primroses and other wild flowers, and two further visits to Studley, one for a flower show put on by the local people and the other when Mary Jane records driving Miss Procter, the Ripon postmistress, and a friend from York, Anna Acton, to see the new Studley Church built by the Marchioness of Ripon. There they heard the organ played by Mr Bentley. "It is a very sweet one" she wrote. "We were especially pleased with the Vox Humana".

This is the only reference in the journal to Mary Jane driving. It would be interesting to know what kind of vehicle it was. On another occasion she refers to riding "Lily". Visits are also recorded to places slightly further afield such as Pateley Bridge, Masham, Bolton Castle and Harrogate. At the latter she records seeing skating "on wheels on boarded floor" and later writes hopefully of a scheme for such a skating rink in Ripon. All the above were just visits for one day, but there were also rather more lengthy local visits; one for a week to Aldfield Spa and two to York where members of her mother's family lived and her father still had friends from his apprenticeship days. On their visit to York in June 1875, she and her cousin Annie (about whom more later) visited a flower show and gala, the museum, a shadow pantomime and "played with Waddie's monkey". They also attended a service in the Minster and afterwards got "stuck on the Minster tower steps behind a very fat woman". It was a very hot summer so to cool down they went on the river where she had "lessons" in rowing. They also witnessed a balloon ascent and saw fireworks. On the second recorded visit to York in 1880 she and Anna Acton decided they wanted to see a Roman Catholic service. On arrival they were told that as they were not Catholics they must pay for a seat. Not wanting to argue, she says, that they were Catholics but not Roman Catholics, they decided on threepenny seats but on finding they were behind a pillar they changed to sixpenny seats in order to get a better view of the proceedings. On this visit to York she also went to the Quaker Meeting House for the marriage of an acquaintance. " After the bridal party came in", she reports, "they sat for fully ten minutes in silence" before first the bridegroom and then the bride rose to affirm their marriage. Other activities were connected with the Assizes. They saw the judges go in procession to the Minster, went to the Mansion House to see the table for the Judges' breakfast and on another day to the Assize Court where they watched twenty minutes of the trial of a poacher accused of wounding a gamekeeper.

The diary also contains accounts of family holidays further afield, to Scarboro', Redcar, the Lake District, Scotland and London. She prepared for the Scottish holiday by reading **The Lady of the Lake** and a history of Holyrood. This holiday had a bad start. They were to set off by the 6.20 am train and she reports "our difficulties began at Ripon - the tourists' tickets which should have been sent from Harrogate yesterday had not come and the booking clerk was late and there was no time to get any tickets of any sort so we went to Thirsk without". She was not too happy either about the journey to London the following year, 1876. She and her father had to wait for 1½ hours in what she calls a "dirty little room at Holbeck", but at least their train did run, unlike ones a few days before - she was writing in April - which had been cancelled because the line was blocked by snow between Grantham and Peterborough. Activities in London included business visits to the London wholesale booksellers and to see a Mr Hughes, a glass stainer, about a memorial window for a Mr Townson. They attended three religious services, one on the Sunday morning at the Temple, one in the afternoon at Westminster and the third in the evening at the Metropolitan Tabernacle where they were disappointed not to hear the famous preacher, Dr Spurgeon, who was indisposed. The rest of the time was spent sight-seeing - she thought the Albert

Memorial "the most beautiful thing of its kind I have ever seen" - going to a concert and a performance of **Alice in Wonderland**, partly by children, partly by magic lantern (did she know of the connection with Ripon?) and shopping, her chief purchases being a New Testament and a French Bible at the Bible Society's depot and some pocket handkerchiefs embroidered by nuns.

It is hardly surprising that accounts of visits form such a large part of Mary Jane's diary. No doubt her life in between was relatively dull. But there were other highlights such as Christmas and birthdays. On her own birthdays she carefully recorded her presents. Amongst these in the period during which she kept her diary were at least two Bibles (one from her brother), a book of poems by Eliza Cook, a bookcase from her father, music, for example a copy of Mendelssohn's **Athalie,** a music carrier, a ring and a ring-stand, a card case, a needle case, a silver and pearl cake knife, a blue bow with a spray of ivy leaves on lace and half a crown - this last from her mother when she had been prevented on one occasion from going out due to bad weather. Her 21st birthday was of course special. Her presents then included a gold watch with a black chain of silk and carved wood from her parents, a music stand from her brother, Henry, and a small japanned cabinet from Sarah Snow. Special gifts apart, Mary Jane's regular 'income' during this period was pocket money of five shillings a month.

On one important occasion Mary Jane records presents given to her parents. This was when they celebrated their silver wedding in September 1875. "Mama received many nice presents. Papa gave her a silver brooch, Auntie a silver fish knife and fork [set?] , Henry a dozen silver dessert knives and forks, Cousin Pattie a silver jam casket, Annie Dinsdale and Eliza Barker an antimacassar each. I worked the lace for a pocket handkerchief and for Papa a slipper holder." After celebrating at home all but Papa went out to Hackfall. One wonders why poor Papa was left out it being his silver wedding too!

Apart from his scorn at the idea of his sister keeping a diary and the various presents he gave her, brother Henry features rarely in Mary Jane's entries. On one occasion he has gone to Harrogate for the annual inspection of the local Volunteer Force of which he was an enthusiastic member and on another to Wimbledon for a national shooting competition. "One point more", she writes, "and he might have got into the last sixty". She also writes that on the latter occasion he had gone to hear Sankey and Moody, the two well known evangelists.

Auntie, who gave Mama a present on her silver wedding day, was Aunt Mary Ann, Mama's younger sister, and Annie Dinsdale was her daughter. As recorded in her brother-in-law's diary, Mary Ann had married Matthew Dinsdale in April 1853. He had been born in Wensleydale but had emigrated to the United States and in 1853 was back in England to fetch his mother, brother and sister. It is not clear whether he had also come back with the intention of marrying Mary Ann or whether the marriage was a by-product of the visit. It would appear that Dinsdale was doing well in America for in 1875 he could afford to send his wife and daughter on an extended visit to England at the time of the Thirlways' silver wedding. Aunt and Cousin had sailed from New York on May 29th on the steamship *Egypt* and arrived in Liverpool on June 8th. They stayed in England until October, most of the time with the Thirlways. Mary Jane was full of admiration for her cousin. "Cousin is very clever" she writes. "She studies at Madison University". When Aunt and Cousin left she was very sad. "The house is so lonely without them. The four months they have been here have been so pleasant. It is so nice to have someone my own age here. Annie is so nice too. I wish I were more like her in decision but I mean to try. I think I am behind other girls of my own age in many things." The visitors had had a good send off from Ripon. "We had quite a levy [sic] last night. Everybody came to say goodbye. It has been a beautiful day. I am glad Annie saw the last of Ripon in the sunshine." Mary Jane and Henry saw the visitors off at Ripon station. Papa and Mama went to Liverpool to see them board the ship for America.

Mary Jane's diary ends in 1880 and we know little of her life after that. She never married. There are a number of references in the diary to a young man called Harry Bowman who asked her to write in his birthday book, and who came twice to say goodbye to Henry when he was leaving Ripon. "I wonder if he thought he would see me too", she wrote rather wistfully. She died in 1910.

NOTES

(1) The Yorkshire Hussars were a kind of 19th century territorial army.

(2) Thomas Gowing, joiner and builder, was a neighbour of the Thirlways at the top of High Skellgate. He was a member of Ripon Corporation in the 1860s and 1870s. Ralph Gowing, his brother, was a plumber.

(3) There was more than one Revd Charnock in the Ripon area at this time. The Revd James Charnock ran a private school at Bishopton Close built for him by Mrs Elizabeth Sophia Lawrence of Studley Royal in 1826 (and since 1874 occupied by the Grammar School). He died in November 1846. The Revd Joseph Charnock mentioned later in these extracts apparently lived at Fountains Hall for a time but the 1861 census shows him at Bishopton Lodge.

(4) The dispensary was at that time in a house in St Agnesgate.

(5) Sulphur waters had been discovered at Aldfield near Fountains Abbey at the end of the seventeenth century.

(6) Procter and Vickers' premises were on the north side of Ripon Market Place.

(7) Stationery with a Ripon Minster letterhead was still being sold by the Thirlways in the twentieth century. At least one sheet has survived in the possession of Mrs M. Thirlway, widow of the diarist's grandson. The letterhead can be seen amongst the illustrations.

(8) This was T. B. C. Smith, the Tory parliamentary candidate in the Ripon bye-election.

(9) The Revd R. L. Sykes assisted the Revd E. Kilvington at Holy Trinity Church (founded in 1827) in its early days.

(10) This was the original Cathedral Boys' School which had been established in St John's Chapel, Bondgate, in 1813.

(11) Thomas Kendall, ironmonger, carried on business on the west side of Ripon Market Place where Boots Chemists now have their shop. He became a councillor in 1840, an Alderman in 1853 and Mayor 1859-60. According to the **Ripon Millenary** Record he was elected Mayor on two other occasions but refused the office. On the first of these occasions he was fined for his refusal.

(12) Shrove Tuesday was by tradition a half-day holiday for apprentices.

(13) The Hon. Edwin Lascelles (1799-1865) was the fourth son of the 3rd Earl of Harewood and M.P. for Ripon 1846-1857.

(14) Wright and Willey had their premises in the Market Place and Durham in Kirkgate.

(15) The Form of Prayer was for a Fast Day called by Queen Victoria because of the Irish Famine.

(16) Digby Cayley lived in St Marygate. In 1839 he was fined for refusing to serve as councillor to which office he had been elected. His son was later twice to be an unsuccessful parliamentary candidate for the Ripon constituency. The Cayleys had a family seat at Brompton Green near Scarborough.

(17) Terry and Harrison's Bank had been established in 1785 and had its premises on the east side of Ripon Market Place. It was later taken over by Bradford Old Bank which eventually became part of Barclays who still carry on business on the site.

(18) Harrison, Judson and Fairburn were all printers and/or booksellers. Their businesses were at 4, 20 and 41 Market Place respectively.

(19) Distributors of Stamps were appointed by the Board of Stamps and Taxes (Inland Revenue). Originally their duties were concerned with the sale of stamped paper for revenue purposes but when postage stamps were introduced it was this Board, not the Post Office, which at first licensed their sale. (Douglas N. Muir : **Postal Reform and the Penny Black**)

(20) "Skins" was a term used in the Post Office and other government boards when referring to the wrapping which enclosed the appointment papers of an employee. The name was probably derived from a clerk's use of real skins to write on or enclose important official records before paper came into everyday use. (Information supplied by Mrs J. Ferrugia, Chief Archivist, Post Office Archives)

(21) See also Note 18. William Harrison was the son of Robert Harrison of Lindrick. He had been apprenticed to John Linney, the Quaker printer, to whose business he succeeded. A member of Ripon Corporation in the 1840s and 1850s he printed important local works and was the local manager of the **Ripon and Richmond Chronicle** to which he was an extensive contributor. His business survives at No. 4 Market Place.

(22) The Right Reverend Charles Thomas Longley, D.D. was the first bishop of the new nineteenth century See of Ripon. He was bishop in Ripon from 1836 to 1856 and was then translated to Durham and later became Archbishop of Canterbury.

(23) The Very Reverend James Webber, D.D. was Dean of Ripon from 1828 to 1847.

(24) Revd R. Poole was a minor canon of the Cathedral. He is probably mentioned in the journal more than any other clergyman.

(25) Revd W. Whiteside was the incumbent of Holy Trinity from 1833 to 1848.

(26) Local festival in honour of St Wilfrid. See **Celebrations** Section.

(27) Revd W. Plues was the Master of Ripon Grammar School for 36 years.

(28) This hall on the south side of Ripon Market Place was the property of the Studley Estate. From its building at the end of the eighteenth century to 1835 the old Corporation of Ripon had been allowed to meet there, but in that year Mrs Lawrence, the owner, was so angered by the provisions of the Municipal Reform Act which altered the constitution of such corporations that she forbade the new Corporation to use the premises. Its use was again permitted in 1851 by the Earl de Grey, heir to Mrs Lawrence. In 1897 the 1st Marquess of Ripon made a gift of the property to the Corporation and it has acted as the Town Hall ever since.

(29) This palace to the north-west of Ripon was sold in 1946 to Dr Barnardo's Homes by the Ecclesiastical Commissioners. It was vacated by Barnardo's a few years ago.

(30) The Riding School, a kind of Drill Hall, was on the site formerly occupied by the Ripon Theatre on the corner of Park Street and Firby Lane, where there is now a bus garage.

(31) Revd W. Gray was the vicar of Brafferton and a canon of Ripon for many years.

(32) Revd P. W. Worsley was rector of Little Ponton in Lincolnshire and a prebend and canon of Ripon for 54 years.

(33) The Misses Maister were the daughters of Major-General Maister J.P., a prominent local landowner who lived in the township of Whitcliffe with Thorpe (Littlethorpe) to the south of Ripon.

(34) The Skellgate Chapel in the Turk's Head Yard off Low Skellgate belonged to the New Connexion Methodists who separated from the Methodist main body in 1796 over their wish for a more democratic constitution for the church. This Skellgate chapel was abandoned in 1860 for a new chapel in Blossomgate.

The chapel in Priest Lane built in 1822 belonged to the Primitive Methodists, another breakaway group. The Primitive Methodists moved to Allhallowgate later in the century.

(35) E. B. Pusey was Regius Professor of Hebrew at Oxford. He was a prominent member of the Oxford Movement which stressed the more traditional aspects of the Anglican Church.

(36) The Socinians were the followers of two reformers who held views similar to those of modern Unitarians.

(37) This was probably the end of the Monitorial System in Ripon (see January 1842).

(38) Mr Thwaites was probably the butcher who occupied the premises next door but one to the Thirlways on the other side of the "Wakeman's House".

(39) The Very Reverend Robert Bickersteth was the second Bishop of Ripon, 1856-84.

(40) The Public Rooms were at the corner of Water and Low Skellgate. They had been established by a company formed by the Reform Party in 1834. They were used by the Mechanics Institute until that organisation put up their own building as explained later.

(41) C. J. Walbran was the younger brother of J.R. Walbran, the noted Ripon antiquary.

(42) Only a few pages later in his journal H.S.T. was writing very appreciatively of another woman lecturer.

(43) This building next to the Public Rooms was sold to the Conservative Club in 1893 when the Mechanics Institute moved into a new building in Finkle Street which is now the Post Office.

(44) W. Williamson was a member of the varnish manufacturing family. He had been Secretary of the Institute for some years and was Mayor of Ripon the year previous to this ceremony.

(45) This latter was George Hudson's proposed branch line.

(46) Fare: 11 shillings. This station was probably Thirsk Junction. Presumably Carlton was Carlton Miniott.

(47) One of George Hudson's lines linked Boroughbridge to Pilmoor on his line running north from York. His idea was to extend this line to Knaresborough and Harrogate with a branch line to Ripon.

(48) Ripon station was ultimately not built on either of these two sites but there is no further mention of the matter in the journal. It seems likely that with the opening of the Ripon to Thirsk part of the line ahead of the line from Ripon to Leeds, the temporary station then required on the north side of the River Ure became a permanent one, thus avoiding further local controversy.

(49) Sir Charles d'Albiac, one time M.P. for Ripon, had died in London on the 8th November 1847. See **People** Section for more details.

(50) See **Thirlway Business** section.

(51) Thomas Cook(e) was the founder of the famous Travel Agency.

(52) This was the Great Exhibition of 1851 held in the Crystal Palace in Hyde Park, London. Many of its six million visitors are said to have travelled by trains on cut-price excursion tickets, large numbers of which were organized by Thomas Cook and others by local societies like the Ripon Mechanics Institute.

(53) Frumenty - a local Christmas Eve dish consisting of a kind of thick porridge made from crushed pearl wheat, soaked overnight and then simmered in milk with sugar or treacle and spices.

(54) Probably the Coltsgate Hill chapel belonging to the Wesleyan Methodists.

(55) John Wood's shop was in High Skellgate. Despite this attempt to end the gift of Yule candles the practice continued into the twentieth century.

(56) St Wilfrid was the Northumbrian monk who helped persuade the Northumbrian Church to adopt Roman rather than Celtic religious customs. It was he who had built the first stone church in Ripon on the site of the present cathedral. The crypt of his church can still be seen. This festival is held in Ripon every year to celebrate his return from exile in Rome.

(57) The Independent Order of Rechabites, a teetotal benefit society, had been founded in 1835. Its name comes from the son of Rechab who founded an order of abstainers from wine: see Jeremiah 35 vs. 6-7. The Independent Order of Oddfellows was a much older benevolent society.

(58) This Temperance Hall was in Allhallowgate and was not the one later opened on Duck Hill.

(59) This passage presents a problem since no evidence has been found of a general celebration of Lammas Day on any other date than August 1st. Though it may seem odd it may be that this problem can be solved by reference to the introduction into England in 1752 of the Gregorian Calendar which was more accurate than the old one, but which meant that eleven days had to be omitted that year. It is a matter of record that in Ripon the Soulmass Fair which had formerly been held at the beginning of November was, because of the calendar change, moved forward to the middle of the month and remained at the later date for about twenty years, so it may be that the same thing happened to Lammas Day, the old English Harvest festival, and so to the Wilfrid Feast which followed it, but with that feast having to wait for nearly a century before it was restored to something approaching the old date for purely secular reasons, as the diarist recounts.

(60) The use of the word 'effigy' here could be an error since the writer has indicated that in 1845 there was already human representation of St Wilfrid, but it could be that there was no established practice for some years. See also the reference to two St Wilfrids on separate dates in 1849.

(61) A rapel is a kind of military drum. Is the use of the expression 'annual tax' to be taken as an ironical reference to donations extracted from onlookers?

(62) Master Henry was Henry Mann Thirlway, the writer's only son, who had been born the previous year.

(63) T.C.Y.M.S. - Trinity Church Young Men's Society.

(64) A halbert is a combined spear and battleaxe. Foresters and Gardeners were two more friendly societies. The Bluecoat School was Jepson's Hospital, the charity school in Water Skellgate, where the City Club now stands. Mrs Lawrence's Hall - the present Town Hall - see note 28.

(65) Canon Dodgson was the father of Charles Lutwidge Dodgson, better known as Lewis Carroll, the author of **Alice in Wonderland.**

(66) Now Morrison's Supermarket.

(67) A picture or series of pictures exhibited a part at a time by being unrolled and passed before the spectator, thus presenting a continuous scene.

(68) A kind of magic lantern show whereby movement brought about by levers and gears gave the appearance of one picture fading (dissolving) into another.

(69) The future 1st Marquess of Ripon.

(70) This presumably refers to the rhyme published in J.O.Halliwell's **Nursery Rhymes of England** in 1842 :
"John come sell thy fiddle
And buy thy wife a gown."
"No I'll not sell my fiddle
For ne'er a wife in town."

(71) Wombwell's Circus.

(72) Whilst piped water was available in parts at least of Ripon at this time its supply was irregular and its quality unsatisfactory, so it seems likely that these watermen carried around water to supplement the piped supplies possibly in leather bags as in the days before piped water was available.

(73) Coal at this time was brought to Ripon by canal. Bondgate Green was at the canal's terminus.

(74) The *Coach and Horses* was in Westgate.

(75) The water works were at Duck Hill, where Skell water was raised to supply the pipes referred to in Note (72) above.

(76) These premises were on the north side of the Market Place.

(77) Thomas Pemberton was a Member of Parliament for Ripon from 1835 to 1843.

(78) A drive three times round the Market Place in a carriage took the place in Ripon during this period of the more informal 'chairing' of the successful candidate shoulder-high shown on some early election pictures.

(79) Charles Oxley was a member of a family who had played a prominent part in Ripon public life since his ancestor came to the city as Master of Ripon Grammar School in 1668.

(80) These dinners were provided by the candidates and their backers for their supporters amongst the electors - only possible of course because electors were still relatively few and voting was public. The writer's father was a strong Tory and had been a councillor since 1841.

(81) The 'League' was the Anti-Corn Law League which was trying to bring about the repeal of the laws imposing a duty on imported corn. The farming interest, of course, opposed this. For Digby Cayley see Note (16).

(82) J. S. Crompton Esq. of Sion Hill, later of Azerley Hall, was a Member of Parliament for Ripon, 1832-1835, and at that time opposed the Tories.

(83) It was only ten years since public elections for councillors had started in Ripon as a result of the Municipal Reform Act. Despite that Act the Corporation had remained very much dominated by the Tory (Studley) interest.

(84) The *Unicorn* belonged to the Studley Estate at this time.

(85) Mr Bayne was a whitesmith with a business in Queen Street.

(86) Captain Smith lived at 'Greenroyd' on the Studley Road.

(87) Sir James Graham had been Home Secretary under Sir Robert Peel from 1841 to 1846. He was Member of Parliament for Ripon from 1847 to 1852. He was to be 1st Lord of the Admiralty under Lord Aberdeen from 1852 to 1855.

(88) There were two separate manorial jurisdictions in Ripon, those of the Archbishop of York and of the Dean and Chapter. These leet courts were the relics of these jurisdictions. Often the only business done was the purely formal recording of the conveyance of customary tenures.

(89) Unpaid constables were still elected by each township but by this time the Liberty of Ripon appointed a paid 'Head Police Officer' who took overall charge of the Liberty constables. The Liberty of Ripon, covering an area which included not just Ripon itself but many surrounding villages, was the relic of an ancient franchise which was still giving the area a degree of independence from the organisation of the rest of the shire.

(For more on this subject see **Ripon Liberty - Law and Order over the last 300 years** by Anthony Chadwick, published by Ripon Museum Trust in 1986.)

(90) 'Cake night' - this may be a reference to the old custom of providing cake and ale to celebrate Charter Day, appointed for the swearing in of the Mayor into his office each year. In fact since 1789 a dinner had been substituted for the cake and ale.

(91) Before the actual poll took place there was a public show of hands in favour of each candidate. Of course many of those present and "voting" were not officially qualified to do so. Thus in this show of hands the vote was always exaggerated in favour of the candidate favoured by the less well-to-do citizens.

(92) The 'Mayor's Dole' was probably what was later, in a Charity Commissioners' Report, referred to as the 'Christmas Dole' paid to poor householders by the Corporation from the proceeds of a number of local charities.

(93) These half-yearly payments were probably those made from the bequests of Alderman John Terry and Thomas Metcalfe to eight poor men and eight poor women of Ripon.

(94) By his will dated 1657 William Underwood left his property near the Horse Fair in Ripon to a charitable trust partly to provide annually £5 to ten poor widows and from the residue 10 shillings each annually to ten poor boys to enable them to be taught reading, writing and arithmetic.

(95) The bathhouse had been built in 1818. It was on the eastern side of the steps which now come down from the Spa Gardens to Skellbank.

(96) Average rents were sums paid to those who lost grazing rights when land was enclosed.

(97) The Maison de Dieu is better known as St Anne's or St Agnes' Hospital - now almshouses and ruined chapel in St Agnesgate.

(98) Thomas Jackson was the librarian and manager at the Public Rooms at the junction of Low and Water Skellgate.

(99) H.S.T. lost his seat in the municipal elections of 1860 and did not seek re-election later.

(100) The Ecclesiastical Commissioners had earlier in the century taken over the collection of the market tolls from the Archbishop of York, Lord of the Manor of Ripon, whose property they had been.

(101) Revd Powell already owned a considerable property in Sharow. The poor lands at Sharow had been purchased by Ripon Corporation with legacies left by Hugh Ripley and Lord John Craven in the 17th century.

(102) According to the Charity Commissioners' Report of 1897-98 the Bishop's purchase was of Dogstile Close which had been part of the land in which the Corporation had invested the money left by Mary Ellis in 1655 to help the poor.

(103) Bull Close was near North Bridge, and Townend Close, as the passage implies, was near the Crescent and adjoining the College.

(104) Pigot's **Directories** of 1841 and 1848 show members of the Carass family as Boroughbridge butchers.

(105) Mr R. Thompson of Blossomgate had horses and gigs for hire.

(106) William Wilberforce, well known as the campaigner against the Slave Trade, was one of the two knights of the shire for Yorkshire in early 19th century parliaments. A considerable property qualification was required for this.

(107) William Langdale was a printer and bookseller with a library and reading room in High Harrogate. He also had an establishment in Knaresborough.

(108) Pickersgill Palliser was the Harrogate postmaster; he also had a bookshop with a library and reading room.

(109) Mr Thomas Church, bookseller, binder and stationer and Mr Thomas Hemsley, saddler and trunkmaker, both had premises in High Street, Knaresborough.

(110) The 1851 census returns show Thomas Fisher, flax spinner, in Mickley. At that time his housekeeper was his aunt.

(111) Henry and John Kirby were flax dressers and spinners, linen manufacturers and bobbin turners at Smelthouse Mill in Nidderdale.

(112) Mr Pinn was probably William John Pinn, a grocer with a business in Kirkgate. His daughters were frequent companions of the Thirlways.

(113) The Ascoughs, like Mr Imeson mentioned later, were related to the writer's wife whom he had married the previous month.

(114) Baines and Newsome were booksellers and stationers of 149 Briggate. From the same address Edward Baines published the **Leeds Mercury** a weekly newspaper which came out every Saturday. Like Baines himself, who had been member of parliament for Leeds during the 1830s, this newspaper supported Whig policies.

(115) Vicar's Croft was at the corner of Kirkgate and Vicar Lane. Leeds street markets for fruit, vegetables etc had been transferred there in 1826. Later in the century the covered Kirkgate Market Hall was built there.

(116) **The Leeds Intelligencer**, like the **Mercury** a weekly newspaper which came out on Saturdays, had its offices at 18 Commercial Street. It supported the Tories. In view of the reference to Adams and Grimshaw which follows immediately after that to the **Intelligencer** it is tempting to conclude that they had something to do with that newspaper but no such connection has been discovered.

(117) Green may have been Walter T. Green, bookseller of 34 Commercial Street, or David Green, bookseller of 166.

(118) Webb and Millington were booksellers of 93 Briggate.

(119) The Commercial Buildings at the junction of Park Row and Boar Lane were funded by a joint stock company and acted as an exchange where merchants could meet to discuss commercial affairs but they also included a coffee room, a restaurant, a concert room/meeting hall, and a fourteen bedroom hotel as well as offices for solicitors, an insurance company etc.

(120) The Coloured or Mixed Cloth Hall and its counterpart the White Cloth Hall had replaced the former street cloth markets in the 18th century. The Coloured Cloth Hall was on the site where later the Leeds General Post Office was built on Kings Square and the White Cloth Hall was on a site between Kirkgate and the River Aire. Designed for the sale of hand-woven cloth they were now in decline because of factory production.

(121) The West Riding Proprietary School in St John's, Wakefield, had been founded a few years before this by a group of proprietors who formed its governing body. Boys were admitted on paying a fee of "not more than £10 half-yearly" and were given either a classical education leading to university or instruction in what were termed commercial subjects.

(122) This property in Darlington is one pointer to the family link with Teesside mentioned in the **Family** section. The property had been bequeathed to the diarist's father and uncle Edward by Ann Snaith of Darlington who described them as her kinsmen in her will drawn up in 1826. It was sold in 1850 by Henry Thirlway and his nephews.

(123) The *Union* was a rival coach to the *Courier* mentioned in a previous extract. It started from the **Wheatsheaf** Inn in Fishergate.

(124) Presumably cousin Henry was employed at the railway works in Wolverton, Buckinghamshire, before going to Manchester.

(125) Alexis Soyer, the famous chef of the Reform Club, had taken over Gore House just outside the Exhibition grounds, redecorated the rooms and reorganised the gardens introducing caves and fountains with illuminations. Here he set up an eating house where the guests were waited on by attendants in sham historical costume. (Reference Y.ffrench **The Great Exhibition 1851**) What is meant by the reference to bells and baskets is not known.

(126) John Tuting, who was of course a close friend of the diarist, eventually returned to Ripon and set up a grocery business in premises next to the ***Unicorn*** in the Market Place.

(127) According to the **Ripon Millenary** Book the two brothers returned to Pateley Bridge legally about 1860. They had acquired money with which they purchased a building known as the old workhouse and the land adjoining it and settled down to peaceful pursuits.

(128) William Grainge in his **Yorkshire Longevity** published in 1864 gives some additional (and some differing) details of George Wharton's life.

(129) The nature of this organization has not been discovered. It seems likely to have been a friendly or temperance society.

(130) 'Devylles' - a nickname for young apprentices in the printing trade who no doubt were frequently covered with ink which made them look like the traditional picture of a devil.

(131) The *Star* Inn was in the Old Market Place and John Pawson's coach probably ran from the ***Angel*** in High Skellgate.

(132) 'Boots' at this time was William Maude, who according to the **Ripon Millenary**, page 182, was employed in that capacity at the ***Unicorn*** for over twenty years. He was eventually killed in an accident at Studley when he had changed his occupation to that of a bus driver.

(133) This Yorkshire Bank is not to be confused with the present one. It was the Yorkshire District Bank, forerunner of the Midland bank, which is at the corner of High Skellgate and Westgate opposite Thirlway's Corner.

(134) Borrage Well is on the west side of the road to Harrogate out of Ripon.

(135) Septimus Tutin, surgeon, lived in Westgate. He was mayor 1843-1844.

(136) "Game at Simon" is presumably the game now sometimes known as "Simon Says" but what is meant by "Salt and Sawdust"? Were they alternative forfeits?

(137) William Farrar was a wine and spirit merchant but nothing is known of a schoolroom in Westgate at this time.

(138) Norton Conyers Hall is to the north of Ripon. It is the home of the Graham family and has associations with Charlotte Bronte.

(139) Daniel, Gowing and Lambert were all plumbers.

(140) This new dispensary which replaced the old one in St Agnesgate was in Firby Lane and is now part of Ripon Hospital.

(141) Dr Robert Paley J.P. at this time lived in Bishopton Grange just to the west of Ripon.

(142) For more about Joseph Barker see **People** Section.

(143) Gas lighting was introduced into Ripon in 1830.

(144) Ripon Grammar School eventually moved from its ancient site in St Agnesgate to Bishopton Close, the property having been presented to the Grammar School by its owner the Marquess of Ripon after the death of Mr Stephenson. Jane elsewhere states that Mrs Stephenson and her eldest daughter subsequently started a school for young children in the city.

(145) The Church Institute occupied rooms in the Town Hall.

(146) At Hackfall, near Grewelthorpe, were gardens in the romantic style developed by the Aislabies of Studley in the later 18th century.

(147) The Band of Hope was a junior branch of the Temperance Movement.

(148) The zenana was the part of the home reserved for women in the Indian sub-continent, so presumably this was a mission to women. When Mary Jane died in 1910 she left £30 to this mission.

(149) Mr Ebdell had his draper's business at No. 17 Market Place.

(150) Mary Jane's work in the Allhallowgate Mission Room was in 1878, but the **Ripon Millenary** records the building as having only been opened in 1879. Perhaps the latter was a rebuilding or a change of premises.

(151) The Temperance Hall on Duck Hill had been opened in 1856. It is now the Small Shops Complex.

INDEX - PEOPLE

In the journal people are often referred to by their surnames only. When there are several people with the same surname, an attempt has been made, by the use of an address or occupation or by the context, to work out to whom the reference is made, but when this has failed the unidentified references have been put together under the surname only.

Abbott, Mr and Mrs	103	Bingley, butcher (York)	25
Acton, Anna	107, 108	Bishop, E.	31
Acton, George	5, 14-15	Blackburn, Godfrey	46, 47, 48, 49
Acton, J.	9, 12	Blackburn, singing boy	55
Acton, T. and Mrs	9, 25	Blacker, John	40, 55, 91
Adam, John	30	Blakeborough, clock maker	100
Adams, Julian	30	Blakey	18, 30
Adams & Grimshaw, Leeds	76, 77, 117	Boots, see Maude	
Addison, John	93	Bowen (London)	83
Allanson, Parsons	20	Bowling Walker & Co. (London)	81
Appleton, J. and W.	2, 80	Bowman, Harry	110
Ascough (Grewelthorpe)	61, 75, 117	Braithwaite	56
Ascough, Marion	9, 117	Brassington, Mr and Miss (York)	
Ascough (Ripon)	65, 117		5, 9, 16, 48, 75
Askwith, A.T.	106	Britain, James	100
Askwith, Lizzie	104	Britain, John	3
Aslin	104	Brown	30, 33, 40
Aspin, family	57	Brown, John, druggist	93
Atkin, Revd	33	Browne, Henry and Thomas	
Atkinson	57		17, 18, 26, 27, 81, 83, 84, 98
Atkinson, fisherman (Redcar)	79-80	Buck, Mr & Miss	7, 8, 49, 57, 59
Auton, apprentice, Harrison's	97	Bunn	49
Auton, grocer	83	Burnett	58
Bailey, Mr and Miss	57	Burton	30, 57
Baines and Newsome (Leeds)	76, 117	Butler, Mr and Mrs	49
Banks	33	Calvert	55
Barker, Elizabeth	109	Cameron (Wakefield)	30
Barker, Joseph	96, 102	Carass, Mrs	18, 48, 73, 117
Barker, Mrs Alice, school proprietress	104	Carlisle, Earl of	70
Barker, Mrs Alice, see Tuting		Carter, watchmaker	60
Barwick, Mr and Miss	33	Catton (Clifton, York)	9
Bateman, Mr and Mrs	40, 70, 72	Cayley, Digby	20, 38, 68, 111
Bates	55	Charnock, Revd James	14, 49, 111
Bayne, W.A.	69, 116	Charnock, Revd John	80
Beckett	71	Charnock, Revd Joseph	16, 80, 111
Bell of Richmond	19	Chipps, bookbinder (London)	81
Bell, H.	31	Church, Thomas, bookbinder	
Bentham, Miss	8, 59	(Knaresboro')	74, 117
Bentley, organist	107	Clymer, Dixon & Co. (London)	19
Bickers, schoolmaster	25	Coates, Matthew	103
Bickersteth, Very Revd R., Bishop of Ripon	28, 72, 106, 113		

Cobbett, William	5
Coldeck	97
Collings, T.	16, 62
Collinson	102
Constantine, butcher	65
Cook, Eliza	109
Cook(e), Thos. (Leicester)	44, 113-114
Cooke, circus owner	48, 49
Copeland, Revd G. (York)	76
Craig, phrenologist	60
Crofts, Revd J. (York)	75
Crompton, J.S.	68, 70, 115
Crow, music teacher	106
Cullock, M.	68
D'Albiac, Sir Charles	40, 67, 95, 113
Dalton, Colonel	95
Dalton, Revd Cecil	75
Daniel, plumber	101, 103, 119
Daniel, Tommy, basketmaker	96
Darnton	30
Dearlove	60
De Grey, Earl	59, 70, 102, 112
Denison	70
Dickens, T.S.	55
Dinsdale, Annie	108, 109-110
Dinsdale, Matthew	109
Dinsdale, Mary Ann nee Mann	8, 9, 12, 45, 109-110
Dixon, schoolmaster	31
Dobson, fisherman (Redcar)	80
Docherhay	57
Dodgson, Revd Canon	53, 115
Douglas	58
Douglas, gig hire	75
Drewell (London)	73
Duckett, contractor	34
Dunnington, Mrs	80
Durham, draper	19, 111
Eardley, Sir Culling	70
Earle, Dr	18, 30
Easter, T.	72
Ebdell, draper	106, 119
Elliott, Captain and family	29, 95
Erskine, Hon. and Revd D., Dean of Ripon	28, 33, 44
Evans, Miss	107
Fairburn, bookseller	21, 112
Fall, Mr and Mrs	57
Farmery, M.	70
Farrar, wine and spirits	101, 119
Fisher, High Skellgate	99
Fisher, J. and T. (London)	81
Fisher, Thomas (Mickley) flax spinner	74, 117
Fisher, Mr, Mrs and Miss	7, 57
Fisher (Thirsk)	107
Fitzwilliam, Earl	70
Fleming, Elizabeth	106
Fletcher (Greenroyd)	93
Fowler (York)	76
Gardener	31
Gardiner, family	57
Gatenby, Dixon	33, 101
Gerhardt's, theatre	60-61
Gibson	58
Gigliardi, circus owner	20
Giles	27
Glaves	31
Goderich, Viscount, 1st Marquess of Ripon	53, 58, 112, 119
Good, the murderer	81, 82
Goodier, Revd and Mrs	107
Gott	30, 55
Gowing, Mrs	93, 101
Gowing, Ralph	101, 103, 111, 119
Gowing, Thomas	12, 19, 72, 111
Graham, Sir J.	26, 69, 116
Grant, Billy	9
Gray, Revd W.	25, 26, 28, 52, 112
Grayson, Revd I.	9
Green, Leeds	76, 117
Greenwood	55
Gregg	48
Grey, Earl	79
Groves, Henry	21
Guy, Mrs, landlady (Redcar)	77, 78, 79
Gyngell	55
Harrison, Henry, bleacher	75
Harrison, Revd T.	75
Harrison (Wakefield)	77
Harrison, William, printer	21, 22, 40, 97, 112
Harrison, William, singing man	93
Hart, Revd S.J.	33
Hartley, Mr and Miss	6, 40, 57
Hartley, Richard	14

Hawkswell, Dick	60
Hebden, Hannah	75
Hemsley, T., sadler (Knaresboro')	74, 117
Hewitson, schoolmaster	25, 26
Hill, Revd J.W.	17
Hirst (the 'Grove')	8
Hodgson, apprentice at Harrison's	97
Holley, Lizzie and brothers	107
Horn, C.	58, 103
Horsefield, George	14, 16, 17, 52
Horsefield, Henry	14, 16, 17, 21, 52
Horsman, Mr and Mrs James	81, 83
Hubbard, Aunty	9
Hudson, George	34, 79, 113
Hudson, Mr and Mrs J.H.	31-32
Huggins (Leeds)	30
Hughes, glass stainer (London)	108
Humphries, John	72
Hunter	57
Husband, Dr	12
Hussey	30
Imeson (Fearby)	61, 75
Ingram, Charles	20, 22
Ireland	40
Irvine	55
Jackson	57
Jackson, apprentice, 'Harrison's'	97
Jackson, grocer	80
Jackson, Public Rooms	72, 116
Jameson, Revd J.	6, 52, 80
Jaques	33, 40
Johnson	33
Johnstone, Colonel	62
Jones, apprentice at Harrison's	97
Jones, coach-owner	98
Jones, Fred (London)	81
Jones, G.B.	71
Judson, William	21, 22, 65, 103, 112
Kearsley, R.	53
Kemble, actor	31
Kendall, Thos, ironmonger	17, 40, 56, 111
Kent, Mrs, confectioner (Sunderland)	79
Kirby, Ed	9, 13
Kirby, Messrs (Smelthouse Mills)	75, 117
Kirk	48
Kohler	30
Lacon	8
Lambe	40
Lambert, plumber	101, 119
Lancaster, John	91
Langdale, bookseller (Harrogate and Knaresboro')	74, 117
Lascelles, Hon. Edwin	18, 68-69, 71, 111
Lawrence, Elizabeth Sophia	5, 59, 93-95, 102, 112
Lewis, Revd W.	28
Leyland, Miss	59
Lidell, printer	18
Linney, John, printer	112
Lofthouse	73
Lomas	33
Longley, Right Revd, C.T., Bishop of Ripon	23, 24, 25, 27, 28, 53, 62, 102, 112
Lovegrove, cab hire (York)	9
Lumley, R.	72
Maister, Misses	26, 112
Malam, gas works contractor	102-103
Mallinson, grocer	83
Mann, Alice Ann, see Thirlway	
Mann, Mr, father of Alice Ann and Mary Ann	8
Mann, Mary Ann see Dinsdale	
Mann, Mr and Mrs J.	9
Mann, W.	9
Marchant, Job	26
Matthew, 'Gas'	20
Maude, William, 'Boots'	98-99, 119
Milburn	33
Mills, H.	9, 13, 76
Mitchell, bookseller (Boro'bridge)	18
Morpeth, Lord	70
Morrison & Co.	81
Mour, Miss	57
Murphy, Sgt-Major	46
Murray, Dr	30, 55
Myalls, London	81, 83
Needell, Mrs	59
Newbald, John	98
Newton, Augustus	71
Nicholson, town clerk	62, 77
Norman, James	30, 40
Nowell, building contractor	100
Nussey	55
Oliver	59
Ostcliffe, Mrs	80

Oxley, C.	66, 77, 99, 115	Richardson, rock, steel and bell band	
Paley, Dr	72, 99, 102, 119		59-60
Paley, shoemaker	71	Richmond Henry	2-3, 74
Palliser, Pickersgill, postmaster		Ricketts, Lady	80
(Harrogate)	74, 117	Ripon, Earl of	34, 53
Parker, F.	71	Robinson	40, 57
Parkin, Miss Elizabeth	6, 8	Robinson, gamekeeper	91
Parkin, Henry and Ben	6, 8	Robinson, John	96
Parkin, Mary Ann, nee Thirlway		Robinson, R., solicitor	20, 21
4, 6-8, 23, 43, 52, 55, 58, 59, 84, 98-99		Robinson, "Unicorn"	99
Parkin, Mary Thirlway	8	Robson, Mrs (London)	81
Parkin, Richard	6-8, 9, 46, 74-75	Rodney, apprentice, Harrison's	97
Partington, Professor	32	Roebuck	70
Paul (Leeds)	52	Roebuck, Methodist preacher (York)	26
Pawson, coach-owner	98, 119	Rollinson, White Horse	68
Pearson (Melmerby)	101	Rose, Revd C. (York)	79
Pell and Co. (London)	81	Rowe	31
Pemberton, T.	66, 67, 115	Rudd, William	21
Pick	78	Sands, Richard	57
Pickard, schoolmaster	75	Sayers, Coach and Horses	8-9, 63, 98
Pinn, Mr and Misses 6, 13, 57, 58, 75, 117		Sergeantson, Miss	26, 98-99
Piper, Wilfrid	73	Shadwick, Revd	23
Plint	68	Sharpin, Haseldine	40, 56, 96
Plues, Revd and Mrs W.	23, 112	Shaw (Laverton)	73, 92
Poole, Revd and Mrs R.		Shawe John	17, 18, 19-20, 21, 27
6, 12, 13, 23, 36, 52, 80, 97, 112		Simpkin, Marshall & Co., London	81, 83
Potts, fisherman (Redcar)	80	Sinkler, Elijah and John	91-92, 118
Powell, apprentice at Harrison's	97	Skinner, bathing machine keeper	
Powell, Revd	72, 117	(Redcar)	77, 80
Pratt, publisher (Stokesley)	77	Skipsey, John Burgess	93
Precious, basket-maker	96	Smith	57
Prentice	68	Smith, Captain	33, 46, 59, 69, 116
Prickett, Revd	36	Smith, John, schoolmaster	5, 96
Prior, Revd H.	73	Smith, T.B.C.	17, 66, 68, 111
Procter and Vickers	17, 111	Snow, Sarah and family	104, 107, 109
Procter, "Green Dragon"	68	Snowden	103
Procter, Miss, postmistress	107	Soyer, Alexis	83, 118
Proctour, apprentice at Harrison's	97	Sparrow	57
Raisbeck, D.	80	Stamp, bathing machine keeper	
Rapers, Miss (Masham)	80	(Redcar)	77
Rattenbury, Methodist preacher		Stapylton, Martin	17
(York)	26	Stead	72
Renton, J.	68	Steel, Matthew and Ann	2, 74, 98
Reynard, C., Hob Green	58, 74	Stephenson, H., Junr	103
Rhodes, Mrs	80	Stephenson, W.F.	104, 119
Richardson, lecturer	33	Stevenson, P.	65
Richardson Revd (York)	76	Strother, George	18, 20, 21, 38
Richardson W.	100	Stubbs, Revd P. (Well)	80

Sunter (Darlington)	55-56
Sutton, Revd	6, 28
Sykes, Revd R.L.	17, 111
Taylor, Richard and family	21
Teasdale, William	1
Telford, R.	72
Terry and Harrison, bankers	20, 111
Tetley (York)	76
Theakstone, family	7
Thirlway, Alice Ann née Mann	8-13, 84, 105, 106,109
Thirlway, Alice Ann, Junr	13,104
Thirlway, Edward, Senr	1
Thirlway, Edward, Junr	1
Thirlway, Henry, father of diarist	2-4, 5,6, 8, 12, 14, 18, 20, 21, 23, 26, 27, 29, 37, 38, 42, 45, 52, 66, 67, 69, 70, 81, 84, 98-99
Thirlway, Henry, cousin of diarist	2, 83, 118
Thirlway, Henry Mann	12-13, 50, 104, 109, 114
Thirlway, James	2, 16, 76, 81
Thirlway, John	2
Thirlway, Mary, mother of diarist	2-3, 7, 8, 12, 23, 45, 52, 73, 93, 98
Thirlway, Mary, aunt of diarist	1, 2, 5, 81, 83
Thirlway, Mary, grandmother of diarist	1, 2
Thirlway, Mary Ann, see Parkin	
Thirlway, Mary Jane	13, 104-110
Thirlway, Thomas	1, 74
Thirlway, William	2
Thomas, Dr	31, 68
Thomas, Revd D. (York)	75
Thompson, Col.	68, 79
Thompson, R., gig hire	18, 60, 73, 117
Thompson, printer (Boro'bridge)	18
Thurlow, Jane née Brown	1
Thurlow, John	1
Thurnell, lecturer	31
Thwaites, butcher	28, 113
Todd, H.W.	29, 31, 61, 81
Townson	108
Trees	103
Trueman, Jane	106
Turner, Sir William	78
Tutin, S.	29, 55, 100, 119
Tuting	57, 58, 59
Tuting, Alice	6-7, 57-58, 96
Tuting, John	9, 34, 39, 40, 91, 102, 118
Tuting, Thomas	7, 28, 38, 79, 80
Underwood, William	72, 116
Van Amburgh, circus owner	56, 57, 73
Vest, Robert, gas worker	103
Vesty	56
Walbran, C.J., J.R. and T.W.	5, 31, 32, 33, 61, 72, 113
Walker (Otley)	18
Walker, railway worker	41
Walker, Sergeants	46
Watson, Sergeant-Major	46
Waytes, Revd J.B.	12, 36
Webb and Millington (Leeds)	76-77, 117
Webber, Very Revd James, Dean of Ripon	23, 112
Wells, W.	72
Wharton, George	73, 92-93, 118
Wharton, Miss	58
Whiteside, Revd J.W.	23, 26, 95, 96, 112
Wilberforce, William	74, 117
Wilkinson, Revd (Redcar)	79
Willan, Revd (Barnsley)	8
Willey, draper	19, 111
Williams (Harrogate)	74
Williams Cooper & Co. (London)	14, 81
Williamson, C. and W.	30, 32, 33, 99, 113
Wilson	57
Wilson (Kirkleatham)	78
Wombwell, circus	60, 115
Womersley	30
Wod, grocer	45, 114
Wood, H.R.	17
Wood, John	71
Wood, Maria Frances	17
Worsley, Revd P.W.	25, 28, 112
Wray, John	95
Wright, draper	19, 57, 111
Yorke, J.	91

INDEX - PLACES

Aldfield	14, 58, 108, 111	Kirkleatham	78, 80
Aldwark near Alne	17	Kirklington	40
Ayton	77	Knaresborough	2, 64, 74, 117
Barnsley	6, 7, 21, 43	Laver, River	14, 61, 97
Bedale	21, 53	Laverton	73, 92
Berwick	12, 84	Leeds	2, 7, 16, 18, 32, 34-44 *passim*, 76-77, 81, 108, 117-18
Bishopton	50, 53, 65, 97, 104, 111, 119	Leith	85
Blyth	17	Leyburn	59
Boroughbridge	8, 18, 19, 38, 73, 113, 117	Littlethorpe	26, 36-43 *passim*, 112
Bramhope Tunnel	34, 39, 43	Loch Lomond	88-89
Brimham Rocks	58, 104	London	2, 5, 18, 20, 34, 81-84, 92, 108-109
Burneston	58	Malton	96
Cambridge	18	Manchester	2
Carlton	34, 113	Markington	73-74
Castle Howard	9	Marske	77
Catterick Bridge	43	Masham	21
Cayton Hall	38	Matlock	7
Clyde, river	88	Melmerby	101
Coatham	77, 79	Mickley	6, 74-75, 117
Copt Hewick	1	Middlesbrough	80
Crimple Valley and Viaduct	40, 42	Monkton Moor	36-41 *passim*
Dacre	23, 25, 75	Newcastle	34, 84
Dallowgill	73	Newhaven, Scotland	85
Darlington	2, 38, 43, 55, 80, 118	Norton Conyers	101, 119
Dishforth	2	Pateley Bridge	91, 118
Edinburgh	12, 84-88, 89-90	Portsmouth, 'Victory'	91
Episcopal Palace	25, 106, 112	Rainton	65
Fearby	61	Redcar	53, 77-80
Fountains Abbey and Hall	16, 18, 43, 44, 93, 95, 111	Richmond, Yorkshire	19
Galphay	21, 98	Ripon Allhallowgate	49, 107, 119
Glasgow	88	Ripon Bathhouse	72, 116
Grantley	2-3	Ripon Black Bull	39, 70, 76
Grewelthorpe	61, 75	Ripon Blossomgate	49, 72, 117
Hackfall	58, 74, 106, 109, 119	Ripon Bondgate	40, 42, 49, 63, 68
Harrogate	34-43 *passim*, 74, 76, 117	Ripon Borrage	100, 119
Hartlepool	5, 80	Ripon Canal (the Navigation)	36-37, 39, 115
Heckmondwyke	18	Ripon Cathedral (Minster)	2, 6, 12, 16, 17, 18, 23, 26, 27, 28, 40, 44, 45-46, 47, 50, 93, 95, 97, 102, 114
Hob Green	74		
Hollin Hall	17		
Hood Hole	19	Ripon Chapels	26, 45, 113
Hovingham	57	Ripon Church Institute	106, 119
How Hill	57	Ripon Closes	72, 117
Hutton	2, 34-41 *passim*, 63, 101	Ripon Coach and Horses	9, 63, 66, 69, 98, 115
Kirkby Malzeard	73, 75, 92, 98		
Kirkcaldy	86		

125

Ripon College	72
Ripon Coltsgate Hill	68
Ripon Court House	34, 40, 44, 71, 99
Ripon Crown and Anchor	55
Ripon Dispensary	14, 96, 101, 102, 119
Ripon Elliott House	95
Ripon Fisher Green	62
Ripon Gas Works	102-103
Ripon Grammar School	104, 112, 115, 119
Ripon Green Dragon	59, 68
Ripon Green Royd	93, 116
Ripon Jepson's Hospital	4-5, 50, 96, 114
Ripon Kirkgate	1, 2, 70, 111, 117
Ripon Lamb Inn	98, 101
Ripon Low St. Agnesgate	111
Ripon Magdalen's Chapel	40, 41, 42
Ripon Maison de Dieu	72, 116
Ripon Market Place	3, 12, 20, 48, 50, 53, 55, 58, 59, 65, 66, 68, 69, 100, 111, 112, 115, 119
Ripon Mechanics Institute	30-33, 113
Ripon Middle Street	2, 3, 100
Ripon National Schools	17, 21, 25, 27, 50, 53, 111
Ripon North Street and Bridge	34, 36, 37, 49, 68, 103
Ripon Park Street	104
Ripon Post Office	65
Ripon Prison	70
Ripon Public Rooms	26, 29-30, 31-32, 52, 55, 60, 98, 113, 116
Ripon Quarry Moor	34
Ripon Racecourse	46-49 *passim*
Ripon Railway	12, 34-44, 108, 113
Ripon Red Bank	5, 53, 93
Ripon Riding School	25, 46, 53, 112
Ripon Royal Oak	98
Ripon Skellgate, High and Low	3, 49, 50, 52, 65, 99, 111, 114, 119
Ripon Skittergate	41-42
Ripon South Parade	47, 62, 100
Ripon Stammergate	64, 111
Ripon Star Inn	98
Ripon Temperance Hall	27, 107, 114, 119
Ripon Terry and Harrison's Bank	20
Ripon Theatre	49, 112
Ripon Thirlway's Corner	3, 4, 6-7, 8, 12-13, 14-22 *passim*, 97, 98-99, 101,104
Ripon Town Hall (Mrs Lawrence's Hall)	25, 52, 53, 62, 68, 70, 102
Ripon Trinity Church	23-28 *passim*, 96, 100, 106, 107, 111, 112
Ripon Unicorn	57, 69, 70, 71, 77 98-99, 115, 119
Ripon Varnish Works	99
Ripon Wakeman's House	96
Ripon Water Skellgate	62-63
Ripon Water Works	64
Ripon Westgate	21, 93, 101, 114, 119
Ripon Whitcliffe	34
Ripon White Horse	68
Ripon Workhouse	66
Ripon Yorkshire Bank	100, 119
Rotherham	21
Saltburn	80
Scarborough	1
Seaton	5, 78
Sharow	36, 72, 117
Sion Hill	115
Skell, river	38-42 *passim*, 62, 63, 93
Skelton	17
Skip Bridge	77
Skipton Bribge	38
Smelthouse Mills	75, 117
Sowerby	42
Starbeck	42
Stockton	2, 43, 80
Stokesley	77
Studley	5, 7, 12, 48, 49, 59, 62, 63, 93, 107
Sunderland	5,78-79
Tees, river and Teesside	1, 5, 78
Thirsk	34-44 *passim*, 77, 91, 98
Ure, River	36-43 *passim*, 62, 64
Wadsworth	17
Wakefield	1, 77, 118
Wakehill	73
Wath	34-40 *passim*, 106
Well	53
Westminster	2, 17
Winksley	74, 101
Witch of the Wood	61
Wolverton	83, 118
York	5-6, 8, 9, 14-16, 25, 43, 75-76, 108